NEW SWAN SHAKESPEARE

GENERAL EDITOR
BERNARD LOTT, M.A., PH.D.

★

The Merchant of Venice

16th | 17th century

poetry   verse

prose for political writing

comical structure.

WILLIAM SHAKESPEARE

The Merchant of Venice

EDITED BY

BERNARD LOTT, M.A., Ph.D.

Longman

Pearson Education Limited,
Edinburgh Gate, Harlow,
Essex CM20 2JE, England
and Associated companies throughout the world

www.longman.elt.com

First published 1962
New impressions *1963; *1964
Second edition (with illustrations) * 1964
Eighty-Eighth impression 2000

ISBN 0-582-52721-X

Illustrated by Ivan Lapper
Cover illustration by Caroline Holmes-Smith

We are indebted to the University of London for permission to reproduce extracts from the English Literature papers of the General Certificate of Education, Ordinary Level.

Printed in Malaysia, TCP

INTRODUCTION

The purpose of this book is to give the text of one of Shakespeare's plays, and to explain it in the simplest way. The text itself is complete; to it have been added notes, a glossary, and an introduction which covers a number of aspects of the play, and there is also a section at the end of the book which gives hints to those who are preparing for an examination on the play. All this additional material will help the reader to get the greatest pleasure from Shakespeare's play – he will find it useful and interesting to know something of the background of *The Merchant of Venice* and its age, of Shakespeare himself, and of drama as an art – but his first duty is to understand what the characters in the play are saying, thinking, and doing, and why they do so.

With this end in view, and to ensure that the help given will in fact simplify the difficulties which are now met with in reading Shakespeare, explanations in the notes and the glossary have been given within the range of a specially chosen list of the 3,000 most commonly used English root-words. Every word in the book which falls outside this list is explained. This is done in the following way:

words which are not used in everyday Modern English as Shakespeare used them, or which are no longer used at all, will be found explained in notes on the pages facing the text; longer passages are also explained there when necessary;

words which are not among the 3,000 root-words of the chosen list, but which are still used in ordinary Modern English with their meanings unchanged, will be found explained in the glossary near the end of the book.

Reference to one or other of these places and a study of section 2 of this Introduction should be sufficient to remove all difficulties in the understanding of the text.

The rest of the Introduction is arranged under the following headings:

1 *The Story of* The Merchant of Venice

Antonio, a rich merchant of Venice, is sad in mind but cannot tell why. Three of his friends meet him and make fun of his mood in the hope that it will disappear, but Antonio remains strangely unhappy. One of his friends, Bassanio, is closer to him than the others, and when these two are left together, Bassanio tells Antonio of his own concerns: he is a gentleman, but he has spent most of his fortune and now wants to go across the sea to woo a rich and beautiful girl called Portia. She has already given him some encouragement, but princely suitors are known to be on their way to woo her, and Bassanio has therefore to compete with them in display if he is to win Portia's hand in marriage. Antonio is very willing to lend him money for the journey, but his own fortune is not at the moment available; it is all in trading ships at sea. He therefore suggests they find out what they can borrow on the open money market in Venice, and readily takes responsibility for seeing that anything lent to Bassanio is paid back. Bassanio approaches a Jewish money-lender named Shylock. Shylock, the Jew, has no liking for Bassanio's friend Antonio, the Christian: Antonio has often insulted him for being Jewish, and has lost him business by lending out money freely, whereas Shylock charges interest. However, Shylock agrees to lend Bassanio money, but on the condition, which he pretends is nothing but a joke, that if the loan is not paid back within a certain time, he will have the right to cut a pound of flesh from whatever part of Antonio's body he may choose. Antonio agrees, and Bassanio is able to set sail for Belmont, Portia's house.

Portia, meanwhile, is being visited by other men wishing to marry her. They each have to submit to a kind of lottery, in accordance with the will of her dead father: they are shown three boxes, one made of gold, another of silver, and another of lead. One box contains Portia's portrait, and the suitor who chooses this one wins her in marriage. The Princes of Morocco and Arragon try their fortune, but each chooses wrongly.

Shylock has a daughter, Jessica, and a servant Launcelot Gobbo. Both are planning to leave him; Launcelot wants to serve Bassanio, and Jessica wants to run away with her lover, a gay young man called Lorenzo. Jessica leaves, disguised as a boy, with a good deal of her father's treasure, and Launcelot is taken into Bassanio's service.

Bassanio chooses the right box and marries Portia. But his happiness is short-lived, for he hears that Antonio's ships at sea have all been lost and that, since the loan cannot now be repaid, Shylock is claiming the pound of flesh. Bassanio hurries away to be with Antonio in his misfortunes, and at the same time Portia arranges, through a famous lawyer who is a kinsman of hers, to go to Antonio's trial dressed as a lawyer herself, and acting on the real lawyer's behalf. She first asks Shylock to show mercy, but he refuses and prepares to cut the flesh from Antonio's body. At that moment Portia warns him that he must spill no blood, and must take no more nor less than just the one pound. Shylock sees that these are impossible conditions, and says he will have the money instead. This, too, is impossible, and in fact the case is turned hopelessly against him because he has committed the crime of plotting to kill a citizen of Venice. The court takes all his wealth away from him, but much of it will go to his daughter.

Jessica and Lorenzo are looking after Portia's house while she is away. At Belmont, when Portia returns, the news is made known that Antonio's ships have, after all, not been destroyed, and that Jessica and Lorenzo are now rich. A little joke which Portia and her maid Nerissa played on their husbands Bassanio and Gratiano (they made them give up their wedding rings, in spite of solemn promises not to do so) is also cleared up, and as morning dawns the play ends happily for all except Shylock.

2 *The Language and Imagery of the Play*

The English of Shakespeare's time was in many ways different from the English we speak today. A good part of all the notes in this book is devoted to explaining these differences in the use of language as they occur in the text. A number of words and forms, however, are characteristic of Shakespeare's English and occur so often in the play that it is better to explain them at once rather than to mention them again and again every time they appear. These words and forms have either changed in meaning since Shakespeare's day, or have fallen out of use altogether in everyday Modern English, or are shortened forms which Shakespeare used for special effects, e.g. so as to fit in with the metrical pattern of the lines.

(No attempt should be made to learn this list by heart; it is to be read through at once and consulted afterwards when difficulties occur which are not explained in the notes.)

adieu – "good-bye".

again – (sometimes) "back".

an – (sometimes, particularly at the beginning of sentences) "if".

anon – "at once".

aught – "anything".

ay – "yes".

become – (sometimes) "suit, look well on".

but – (sometimes) "only".

do, does, did are often used with another verb, but without adding any separate meaning; e.g. "How shall I know if I *do* choose the right?" (II.vii.10).

e'er – "ever".

enow – "enough".

ere – "before".

ever – (sometimes) "always".

exeunt (Latin) – "they go out", i.e. leave the stage.

exit (Latin) – "he, she goes out".

faith, in *in faith* or *i' faith* – "indeed".

fare . . . well (e.g. *fare ye well*) – "good-bye".

fie, an exclamation expressing disgust.

forth – "out and away".

hence – "from this place".

hither – "to this place".

how now! – "hallo!; what news?"

i' th' – "in the".

marry! – an exclamation, "(By the Virgin) Mary!"

methinks – "it seems to me; I think".

mine – (sometimes, particularly when the following word begins with a vowel) "my".

morrow, in *good morrow* – "good day", a greeting.

nay – "no".

ne'er – "never".

o'er – "over".

oft – "often".

pray, as in *I pray you* – "please".

presently – "at once".

sirrah, a form of address used to servants.

still – (sometimes) "always".

straight – "at once".

tarry – "stop; stay".

–th sometimes appears instead of *-s* as the ending of verb-forms in the third person singular, present indicative; e.g.

"Who choose*th* me shall gain what many men desire" (II.vii.5).

thither – "to that place".

thou, thee, thy, thine – "you, your, yours (singular)".

These forms are often used for the second person singular pronoun, particularly in speaking to a servant, relative or close friend. Old Gobbo uses *you*, etc., in speaking to Launcelot until he is sure that Launcelot is his son; then he uses *thou*, etc.:

I cannot think *you* are my son . . . .

I'll be sworn, if *thou* be Launcelot, *thou* art mine own flesh and blood. (II.ii. 77, 80–1)

The verb associated with *thou* as subject ends in *-st* or *-est*, e.g.

How do*st* thou and thy master agree? (II.ii.88–9)

The verb *to be*, and one or two others, however, are irregular in this respect, e.g.:

Lord, how *art* thou changed! (II.ii.88)

thrice – "three times".

't – "it", e.g. in *'t was* – "it was".

troth, in *by my troth* – "indeed".

unto – "to".

whither – "to which place".

withal, a strong form of *with*, used at the end of a sentence.

wont – "accustomed".

would – (sometimes) "wish".

yea – "yes".

yon, yonder – "(situated) over there".

Shakespeare was a poet, and, like all poets, he employed language in a way which is not usual for the making of direct statements in prose. There is much beautiful poetry in *The Merchant of Venice* – the speeches of Lorenzo in the last act are strikingly lovely in words and poetic rhythms – and most of it is written not as prose but in lines of verse. These lines generally follow a fixed pattern of stressed and unstressed syllables; e.g.:

> This bond doth give thee here no jot of blood;
> The words expressly are "a pound of flesh" . . .
> (iv.i.302–3)

This is an example of the usual arrangement in Shakespeare's plays, where the rhythm depends upon five stressed syllables in each line, separated from one another by unstressed syllables. But completely regular rhythm would be very dull to listen to, and Shakespeare avoids it in a number of ways, such as by varying the positions of the stressed syllables in the lines; e.g.:

> Therefore thou must be hanged at the state's charge.
> (iv.i.363)

and by making a rhythmic stress fall lightly on what would, in ordinary speech, be an unstressed syllable; e.g.:

> But in the cutting it, if thou dost shed . . .
> (iv.i.305)

where *in* is so treated. Again, he sometimes puts more unstressed syllables into a line, particularly at the end of it, than the normal pattern requires; e.g.:

> It is enacted in the laws of Venice (iv.i.344)

where -*ice* in *Venice* is one syllable more than in the basic pattern. Occasionally the lines rhyme in couplets (i.e. two lines next to one another), particularly at the end of a scene or of a long speech within a scene. An example is:

> Bid your friends welcome; show a merry *cheer*—
> Since you are dear bought, I will love you *dear*.
> (iii.ii.310–11)

The question may well be asked: since in ordinary life people do not speak in poetry, what was Shakespeare's purpose in making most of his characters do so? The answer is that by using poetry Shakespeare could make his characters say more effectively what he wished them to. Poetry is often more precise and carries more meanings along with it at one time than prose can usually do. The swing of the rhythm in lines of verse moves the play along quickly and pointedly. Lorenzo could certainly have talked *about* music in the last act if he had spoken only in prose, but when he speaks as he does with the aid of poetry his words have a music of their own which beautifies and perfects the subject they treat of:

> There 's not the smallest orb which thou behold'st
> But in his motion like an angel sings,
> Still quiring to the young-eyed cherubins.
>
> (v.i.59–61)

The poetic use of language is also characterized by imagery, which adds to ordinary statements visions of something different but at the same time similar in some respects. Imagery may be expressed by the use of simile or metaphor.

A *simile* is a direct comparison between the subject treated and the image which that subject recalls; e.g., Bassanio says of Portia:

> her sunny locks
> Hang on her temples like a golden fleece,
>
> (i.i.168–9)

and by doing so makes a comparison between her golden hair and the golden wool of the sheep in a classical story (see note 81, page 12, for a full account of this). This mention of the golden fleece leads him to think of Jason, the hero who won it after many difficulties, and with it a kingdom that was his right. It

> makes her seat of Belmont Colchos' strand,
> And many Jasons come in quest of her. (i.i.170–1)

A *metaphor* is a comparison which is only suggested, not made directly. Words used metaphorically refer at once to two or more different things, usually recalled together in moments of strong feeling. The matter of the golden fleece, as shown above, leads Bassanio to speak of Portia's suitors as Jasons; he does not say that each is, like Jason, in some way or other contending for a rich golden prize, but that they *are* Jasons, and the listener must think out for himself in what respects this is so. The interest of

xi

this imagery is increased when other references to the same image are made as the play goes on. The story of Jason is a good example; Bassanio is successful in winning Portia's hand in marriage, and Gratiano succeeds in winning her maid Nerissa. It is Gratiano who now says:

> I know [Antonio] will be glad of our success;
> We are the Jasons, we have won the fleece.

Salerio takes up the word *fleece* and uses it to mean Antonio's wealth at sea, perhaps with a pun on *fleets* (see notes 127 and 128, p. 130):

> I would you had won the fleece that he hath lost.
>
> (III.ii.238–40)

The imagery here has made a kind of pattern; it binds the wooing and the success as they are bound up in the story of Bassanio's venture.

There are many other examples of imagery in the play. At the beginning the talk runs on ships at sea, since Salerio and Solanio suggest that Antonio's sadness might be due to worry over his merchant-ships. Salerio says:

> Your mind is tossing on the ocean,
> There where your argosies with portly sail,
> Like signiors and rich burghers on the flood,
> Or as it were the pageants of the sea,
> Do overpeer the petty traffickers. (I.i.8–12)

Later, when the masquers are waiting for Lorenzo to come for Jessica, the conversation turns to the ways in which pleasures, however great, fall away in the end. Gratiano gives one or two examples of this to pass away the time while they are waiting, and finishes with the image of a great ship setting out proudly at the beginning of a voyage, and returning at the end in bad condition,

> With over-weathered ribs and ragged sails,
> Lean, rent, and beggared by the strumpet wind!
>
> (II.vi.18–19)

This, or worse, is what Antonio fears has happened to his ships. Further, Gratiano likens the ship to a prodigal; Bassanio, the source of much of Antonio's worry, has something of the prodigal in him.

In *The Merchant of Venice*, poetry is the means by which all except the humblest characters normally express themselves. When other characters use prose, their feelings are less strong than when they speak in verse. When Portia and Nerissa are talking privately about the suitors, they use only prose (i.ii). Shylock says a good deal in prose, as when Bassanio asks him for the loan and he thinks over the proposal (i.iii; Bassanio is very impatient here and speaks to Shylock quite informally), and when Solanio and Salerio tell him the latest news of Jessica and Antonio (iii.i). Launcelot Gobbo and his father, the amusing characters of the play, invariably talk in prose. This signifies their humble origins; they talk like this because Shakespeare's poetry is not a mode of expression for funny scenes. Even when Jessica talks to Launcelot in verse he replies in prose:

> Adieu! tears exhibit my tongue, most beautiful pagan, most sweet Jew! . . . these foolish drops do something drown my manly spirit; adieu! (ii.iii.10–11, 12–13)

One other feature of the play should be noticed: there are many references to, and echoes of, passages from the Bible. It seems that in this play they are deliberately introduced as a kind of contrast to the anti-Christian language of Shylock. Launcelot, Shylock's servant, is particularly fond of using such echoes in front of his master, no doubt to annoy him, but they also occur quite frequently elsewhere.

3 *The History and Background of the Play*

Shakespeare wrote *The Merchant of Venice* a year or two before the end of the sixteenth century. It is mentioned by name in 1598, and one or two references in it have been studied as a possible means of giving the earliest date at which the play could have been written. The most important of these is the reference to a ship as "my wealthy Andrew" (i.i.27). In 1596 a Spanish ship called the *St. Andrew* ran aground in the harbour of Cadiz and was captured by English seamen. She was bigger than the English merchant ships and was consequently often in danger of running aground again, particularly off the eastern shores of Britain. There is little doubt that Shakespeare had this incident in mind when he made Salerio imagine he saw "my wealthy Andrew docked in sand".

Some scholars have suggested that Gratiano's words about "a wolf . . . hanged for human slaughter". (IV.i.134) may likewise refer to an incident in history. In the play, Gratiano is expressing his bitter hatred of Shylock; Shylock, he says, almost persuades him to believe in Pythagoras' theory that the souls of animals when they die can move into the bodies of human beings. If this is so, he continues, the spirit of a murderous wolf must have moved into Shylock's body before he was born. In 1594 Roderigo Lopez, a Portuguese Jewish doctor who was physician to the reigning Queen Elizabeth I, was accused of plotting to kill the queen. The accusation seems to have come from the Earl of Essex, who disliked Lopez and was also most probably jealous of the power he might have had over the queen. Essex headed the court at the trial and Lopez was found guilty (probably unjustly) and afterwards hanged. There was, then, a notable trial of an important Jew near to the time that the play seems to have been written. It has been suggested, further, that Gratiano's mention of *wolf*, which is in Latin *lupus*, would remind people of Lopez, particularly since Lopez was popularly known in English as *Lopus*. But this theory is no longer widely accepted. Gratiano may simply be referring to the fact that wolves were hanged for killing sheep in Elizabethan times; he is certainly thinking of a wolf, not a man, when he mentions this. The speech should probably not, therefore, be taken as evidence from which to date the play. Shakespeare almost certainly wrote the play, then, at some time between the summer of 1596 and that of 1598.

Even though the connection between these two incidents and the play cannot be proved, the mention of them here serves as an illustration of the kind of event which people experienced in the age of Shakespeare. Shakespeare, as an actor, wrote his plays for the people of his own age, and knew that they would be a mixture of types, the rich and poor, the quiet and noisy, the proud and humble – it was these people he wanted to please, not the generations of play-goers who followed them.

The lives of these people were in many ways very different from those of English people today. For one thing, the contrasts among the audiences at the theatres of Shakespeare's day reflected the conditions of their age. Life was at once gay and cruel, very comfortable for the rich and still bad for the poor. The rich, like the queen herself, loved fine clothes, yet there were beggars who had scarcely enough to cover themselves. Many people enjoyed using their language in speeches, writing and poetry, yet this language could sometimes be used for most unworthy ends. England had recently become the most powerful nation in the world, and this position brought at once a dislike and mistrust of foreigners, yet a new spirit of adventure sent seamen to discover new lands in distant parts of the earth.

What united the nation was loyalty and devotion to the person and power of the queen. During her reign, the Church of England became permanently set up with the queen herself at the head. She dealt cruelly with the few, such as the Roman Catholics, who opposed her in this, but the vast majority of the nation was behind her and she became the champion of all Protestants in Europe. Even the Jews could not legally settle in England without making some denial of their faith. A part of the penalty Shylock has to pay in Venice is to "become a Christian" (IV.i. 383). The queen's foreign policy was mainly directed against the Roman Catholic nations, particularly France and Spain, since it was thought that those nations planned to interfere openly in English affairs. And such was the queen's skill in government that open war was avoided from 1558, when she came to the throne, until the sea-power of Spain made an all-out attempt to challenge the English naval forces in 1588. A great Spanish naval force, the Armada, was destroyed off the English coast, and England was afterwards safe from foreign interference in both politics and religion.

Elizabeth never married – she said she had "married England" – and, though a woman, ruled her country with strength as well as wisdom. At home she took the greatest interest in the welfare of her people, seeing ways to help the poor by providing them with work and the necessities of life, and having about her a splendid court of brave and clever men prepared to fight for her and entertain her. As England became richer, particularly as a result of the discovery of new lands, the standards of life rose; this was shown in better housing for the people, finer household articles, richer clothing, and a rise in learning among the common people. With this, too, came more leisure time, particularly for those associated with the courts of the queen or the great nobles. It was this leisured class which cultivated the arts, including poetry and drama, and Shakespeare was supreme among them. Like Portia's Belmont, a great house would have its own group of musicians as well as numbers of servants, beautiful gardens and a library. To the house were invited writers and adventurers who would tell the noble people how they spent their time and would bring with them an atmosphere of interest in the arts, such as writing, painting and music, and in new lands across the seas.

One interest which appealed to high and low alike was the play. Drama in England before Shakespeare was of two kinds. One was particularly associated with the court, the great houses and the universities. There was also a popular drama, religious for the most part, which continued to be presented in public places to entertain the passers-by. However, by the time Shakespeare was writing his great plays, theatres, buildings especially put up for the performance of plays, were already open in London and had become very popular.

To enjoy *The Merchant of Venice* fully, it is very necessary to remember that Shakespeare wrote it not to be read but to be acted, in a theatre of his day, and for the entertainment of the people he saw around him. The play cannot live fully until one imagines how the actors must look on the stage, listens to what they say, and sees what they do. If at all possible, the best way to begin a study of the play is to see it acted. But students can go some way towards this by taking every opportunity to speak the lines aloud for themselves rather than just reading them silently. They may not have any skill as actors, nor may they have the time or ability to learn long speeches by heart, but it is always worth reading parts aloud together, or staging some striking scenes (even if this means acting with book in hand). In this way a stage performance can most easily be imagined.

One cannot go very far in such an active presentation of the play without realizing that the theatre for which it was written differed in some ways from the theatre we know today. Elizabethans loved splendid language, high-sounding words and powerful speeches, and Shakespeare wrote for them in this way. Such effects were particularly necessary for passages of description, because the plays were acted in daylight and with very little scenery, perhaps none at all, so that the producer had to rely upon good speech much more than anything else to catch the interest of his audience. And to set the scene it was necessary for the characters to talk of it themselves in a way most likely to interest the audience. It seems that Shakespeare, realizing this, brought his finest poetic powers to bear on some of the descriptions needed in his plays. In *The Merchant of Venice*, a number of the best-loved passages are of this sort; they can be somewhat detailed, as when Lorenzo calls Jessica's attention to the beauties of the gardens of Belmont at night and the starry sky above them:

> How sweet the moonlight sleeps upon this bank!
> . . . Sit, Jessica. Look how the floor of heaven
> Is thick inlaid with patens of bright gold . . .
>
> (v.i.53, 57–8)

or the effect can be achieved by simple means:

> The moon shines bright.

or:

> That light we see is burning in my hall.
> How far that little candle throws his beams!
>
> (v.i.1, 88–9)

For Shakespeare's theatre everything depended upon the words in these and similar passages, since neither moonlight nor a distant candle-flame could be seen in the daytime.

In Shakespeare's day the playhouse stage stretched far out into the open space where the audience sat or stood – so far, in fact, that they were gathered round three sides of it. The fourth side extended back a considerable way, and formed a recess which was roofed over by a second floor. A good deal of action could take place on this upper floor. It was certainly used, for example, by Jessica when in the play she appears "above" and calls down to Lorenzo waiting below, ready to take her away. She throws him some of her father's treasure, then hurries down to join her lover below (II.vi.26ff.); and so they make their escape with the masquers. The recess beneath was covered with a curtain when not in use. It was a suitable place in which to keep the caskets for the suitors' lottery:

> Go, draw aside the curtains and discover
> The several caskets to this noble prince (II.vii.1–2)

says Portia to her servants.

This kind of stage was very suitable, too, on the occasions when a character speaks "aside", i.e. to himself, so as to let the audience know what he is thinking, or speaks directly to the audience. Such passages often occur in Shakespeare's plays; and in his time the actor who was to speak them could walk to the front of the stage, in close contact with the audience, but at a distance from the other actors. It was, therefore, easy to suppose that they could not hear him, and it was unnecessary for him to speak in other than his ordinary voice. An excellent example of this occurs when Shylock says what he thinks of Antonio the merchant:

> How like a fawning publican he looks!
> I hate him for he is a Christian . . . (I.iii.34–5)

The stage was also big enough to give room for a good deal of movement, numbers of actors passing to and fro in gaily-coloured costumes. A good opportunity for this kind of display is offered when the princely suitors come to try their luck with the caskets. Even though there was little or no scenery, the costumes worn by the actors could make a fine show; the Prince of Morocco, dressed in white to bring out by contrast the dark colour of his skin, enters with his followers on one side of the stage, while Portia and Nerissa, dressed as the great lady and her most favoured maid, come in with their train on the other. And at the same time the trumpets play a flourish from the upper stage. This made the kind of display that the Elizabethans loved.

The action of the play is supposed to take place in Venice and the district near by (apparently across a short stretch of sea). There is no indication that the time which it is meant to represent is before Shakespeare's own day. This being so, scholars have pointed out a number of places where the details of description are not according to the facts. But such matters are of no importance; Shakespeare's purpose was not to describe Venice but to tell a story through speech and action on the stage. For the setting and the age he took what he needed, often very accurately, and paid no attention to what he did not. For instance, he knew that Padua (Padova), where there was a university famous for law studies, lay near to Venice, and to get there one had to cross a river. Portia, when she sends a letter to her cousin Bellario telling him how she proposes to dress up as a judge, orders Balthazar to take

> this same letter,
> And use thou all th' endeavour of a man
> In speed to Padua . . .
> Bring [the notes and garments Bellario gives you], I
>   pray thee, with imagined speed
> Unto the traject, to the common ferry
> Which trades to Venice. (III.iv.47–49, 52–4)

For the purposes of the play it is unimportant to know, for instance, that there were many Jews in Venice at the time, and that an enquiry such as Old Gobbo's about "the way to Master Jew's" (II.ii.32–3) would therefore be foolish, or that the Duke of Venice (the Doge) and the rich merchants of the city did not attend the courts of justice. No court of justice there, or perhaps anywhere else, would have passed judgement on the play of words which resulted in Shylock's downfall, but that is the kind of detail which must be accepted in the story. At least the moonlit night is an Italian one, warm enough to sit out in until the early morning and watch the moonlight playing on the grassy banks.

4 The Construction of the Play

Shakespeare's main source for the story of *The Merchant of Venice* was an Italian tale taken from a collection named *Il Pecorone*, by a writer who calls himself "Ser Giovanni". It was first written at the end of the fourteenth century, and Shakespeare may have read it in a printed edition in Italian, or in an English translation of which no trace remains. There is some evidence to suggest that he could understand Italian; certainly a number of his plays come from Italian sources, a fact which accounts for so many of them having characters with Italian names. Again, the flowering of English art referred to above was in some ways inspired by the great Italians; in particular, Italy was looked upon as the home of story-telling, and many Italian stories were known and enjoyed in England. The story in *Il Pecorone* has in it the two main plots of Shakespeare's play, the wooing of a great lady and the attempt of a Jew to take the flesh of a Christian when a loan is not repaid. The details of the wooing are quite different from those in *The Merchant of Venice*, although the hero has to borrow money through his godfather (as Bassanio borrows through Antonio) in order to visit the lady. But the flesh-bond plot is very similar; it includes the lady appearing in court disguised as a lawyer, the trick by which the pound of flesh cannot be forfeited, and the joke about the ring.

Some other, less important, sources have been noticed: Shakespeare probably got some suggestions for Portia's speech on mercy (IV.i.180ff.) and some of the ideas about money-lending, from Anthony Munday's *Zelanto or the Foundation of Fame* (1580), even though here the usurer is a Christian; he is certain to have known Christopher Marlowe's play *The Jew of Malta*, and uses words which remind one of it; the story of the caskets is a very old one, and Shakespeare may have read it in an English translation of the *Gesta Romanorum* ("Acts of the Romans").★

Perhaps the most important thing that comes out of a study of these sources is the realization of how much greater Shakespeare's work is than any of them. His characters are more individual and their words fuller in meaning, and he has made the stories immediate by knitting them together and presenting them alive on the stage. Even when events happen which cannot be repre-

★ Copies or translations of these sources can be seen in the appendices to John Russell Brown's admirable edition of the play in the *Arden Shakespeare*, London, 1955, pp. 140 ff.

sented there, such as the secret journey of Portia and Nerissa from Belmont to Venice, they are explained clearly enough, and yet shortly too, for immediate appreciation. This comes largely from Shakespeare's skill in arranging the materials of his plot. And it is to the construction or pattern of the play that we now turn.

The incidents are arranged so cleverly that not all scholars agree as to the underlying principle of construction. Only one pattern will be suggested here, not because it is necessarily the only correct one, but because it is sufficient as one way of seeing the play as a whole. There are others, perhaps, equally good, but in the end they, too, will serve only this same purpose, to show how the arrangement of the incidents makes a complete and satisfying play.

Antonio, the Christian, and Shylock, the Jew, are in opposition, even while the loan is being arranged, but they have some things in common: both are outside the happiness that the other main characters enjoy; both are lonely, and destined to suffer. And both, in a strange way, are lovers: Antonio loves Bassanio (his friends tease him when he first appears by saying he is in love, but that is not true in the normal sense), and when his end seems very near he thinks only of Bassanio; he says to him:

> Say how I loved you, speak me fair in death;
> And when the tale is told, bid [your wife] be judge
> Whether Bassanio had not once a love. (IV.i.271–3)

Shylock loves riches more than anything else, even his daughter:

> I would my daughter were dead at my foot, and
> the jewels in her ear. (III.i.71–2)

The play is about these two "outsiders" coming into opposition with one another. On the face of it, Shylock's love of riches is just the thing to help Antonio further his dear friend's wishes. Although Shylock makes some apparent difficulties about giving a loan, there is never any real doubt that it will be effected. The rest of the play is mainly a study of this relationship, the Jew's desire for revenge and the Christian's patient acceptance of fate.

Who is to be satisfied? For a long time it seems certain that Shylock will be; but by a dramatic turn Antonio goes free and Shylock is ruined.

Shakespeare fits the other material into this framework with great skill and apparent ease. Bassanio cannot return Antonio's intense love (though he pretends he can, as when he says:

> Good cheer, Antonio! what, man, courage yet!
> The Jew shall have my flesh, blood, bones and all,
> Ere thou shalt lose for me one drop of blood.
> (IV.i.111-3))

and if love were given according to worth he would hardly be worthy of it; but in any case his love is all Portia's, and we see how he woos and wins her. She has a maid who is loved by the fiery Gratiano; he, too, woos her successfully, but both he and Bassanio must suffer a comic set-back over the matter of the rings. The Gobbos are another link between the two main characters; Launcelot moves from one side to the other when he changes masters. The love between Lorenzo, Bassanio's friend, and Jessica, the Jew's daughter, is yet another link. On Shylock's side the seeming certainty that he will get his revenge does not go towards improving his relations with his fellow men. His daughter and his servant leave him, and even Tubal plays with him instead of acting towards him as a true friend, raising his hopes when they are down and throwing them down when they are raised again. At the end of the play the lovers move off happily in music and moonlight, having laughed over the jokes of the rings; the Jew is ruined as a punishment for his desire of revenge; Antonio is rich again, but somehow remains outside the happiness of the rest; while they are talking and laughing with joy at the prospect of loving marriages, Antonio's words, almost his last, are:

I am dumb.

5 The Characters

Antonio, the merchant of Venice, shares with Shylock the central place in the play, and it is to him that the title refers. He is known to be rich, generous, and helpful to those around him, and has, in fact, been especially kind to Bassanio before the play opens. With others he may be formal in manner, but with Bassanio he can talk freely, even about such delicate things as Bassanio's love for the lady Portia. And to go to her again Bassanio needs money, which he is eventually able to borrow from Shylock, with Antonio agreeing to be responsible for him. Antonio enters into what Shylock calls a "merry bond", by which, if the loan is not paid back within a certain time, Shylock can take a pound of Antonio's flesh instead. Events move quickly; we hear that Antonio has suffered losses at sea and will not be able to pay back the debt at the time agreed, but he is not seen again until the day before he must face Shylock in court. He meets Shylock on his way to prison, and pleads with him for a little longer time to pay in; but Shylock will not listen, and Antonio is led away, hoping only that Bassanio will be there when he must face death from the Jew's knife.

In the court Antonio is ready to submit quietly to his fate, since his case seems to him hopeless. He asks only that judgement should be pronounced quickly, and it is evident that Shylock will not accept any money, even though it is now available, because he wants what is his by law. Antonio has something about him which reminds us of the Christian sacrifice:

> I am a tainted wether of the flock,
> Meetest for death. (IV.i.114–5)

A stranger is announced, a young lawyer from Padua and a clerk with him. The lawyer recommends that Shylock should be merciful, but he refuses; and then, by reference to the word rather than the spirit of the bond, this clever young lawyer quickly turns the case in Antonio's favour. Antonio then says very little. Asked what mercy he is prepared to show to the Jew, he thinks of how Lorenzo and Jessica can use Shylock's riches, and demands that Shylock should become a Christian. He then thinks of how the lawyer and his clerk can be rewarded, and his part is done when he accepts responsibility for causing the trouble about the rings, and hears without passion that his ships are, after all, safely returned.

The character of Antonio has a tragic beauty, the charm of a person who is sad by nature, quiet and kindly. Most of us feel we want to help people like Antonio, since there is something strangely helpless about them. For Antonio even good luck smiles rather sadly, and his manner suggests that some unpleasant fate is waiting near by to take him off. Only Shylock hates him for his kindness to those who ask him for money, and because of this Antonio reasonably hates him in return – and such hatred is perfectly in character, because Antonio is nowhere afraid to look facts in the face. If his way with Shylock is too harsh to win all our sympathy today, it would not have seemed so to Shakespeare's audience, among whom pity for the sufferings of ordinary people was less developed. What we see in Antonio is a wealthy man in whom there is no greed; it is in this that he contrasts most plainly with Shylock. Antonio is as frank in his giving as in his friendships, and it is reasonable that he should be like this too in his hatred of the man who mocked at his acts of kindness and hated him for them.

Shylock is not, like Antonio, the mainspring of the plot, but he is the character in *The Merchant of Venice* which people most often remember, because he is so striking, original and many-sided. He is a Jew, and a money-lender by profession. It is to him that Bassanio goes when he needs to borrow money for his journey to Belmont, and Antonio agrees to be responsible for repayment of the loan. Shylock thinks over the proposal with great care (in contrast to Bassanio, who is in a hurry to have it agreed), and wants to see Antonio first. But he will not see him at dinner; instead they meet in the street. Shylock expresses his hatred of Antonio as a Christian and as a merchant who lends out money without charging interest on it. And he makes much of the fact that Antonio, who has often treated him with contempt, now wants to borrow from him. At last he agrees, on the condition that, if the money is not paid back at a certain time, Antonio will have to forfeit a pound of his flesh. Bassanio does not like the arrangement at all, but Antonio accepts. Shylock loses his daughter to a Christian lover, and his servant goes over to the very man to whom he is lending money. He rages more over the loss of the riches Jessica has taken with her than over his daughter herself, and even tries to search the ship which Bassanio has boarded for the voyage to Belmont in case she and her lover are there. He also sends out Tubal, a friend of his, to look for her. But the news that Antonio may have lost some ships pleases him, because he hopes to get the forfeit of the bond, and to this end he tells everyone concerned that after the agreed day he will accept no money but only Antonio's flesh.

Antonio fails, and news of it reaches Bassanio at Belmont. Portia has a plan to help Antonio, but says nothing of it to Bassanio, so that when Antonio appears in court, charged with failing to pay his debt, his case seems hopeless. Shylock is determined to get his penalty, and when asked to explain why, he says it is a fancy, like other people's. A strange young lawyer, Portia in disguise, is called in; "he" asks Shylock to be merciful but Shylock refuses. The lawyer then pretends that nothing can help Antonio, but when everything seems to be going in Shylock's favour, a difficulty is brought up: he must not spill any blood and must take exactly one pound of flesh. He sees at once that this condition is impossible and, being a business-man, he says he is prepared to accept the money offered. But he cannot have this because he has already refused it. The phrases he has used to praise the strange lawyer – "O wise and upright judge"; "A Daniel come to judgement" – are mocked by Gratiano, and Shylock in his rage wishes only to leave. But now he ought by law to lose his life and property, because, as an alien, he has attempted to kill a citizen of Venice. The Duke spares his life, and it is arranged that Jessica and Lorenzo should profit from his riches; then he is free to leave, but first he has to promise to become a Christian. Mercy has been shown to him where he showed none, and we do not see him again.

There can be no doubt that Shakespeare intended us to consider Shylock as a villain, but Shakespeare was too clever a playwright to make him all black. Indeed, there are places where he is very near to winning our sympathy. He is carrying on a business, money-lending, which Christians in Shakespeare's England considered to be wicked, but which they could not manage without. He is therefore doing necessary work which others are morally afraid of doing; and, to judge from his riches, he is doing it well. Nor could he help being born a Jew; many people have been moved by his speech on a Jew's humanity being the same as a Christian's (III.i.46ff.). He is faithful to his race, and for it he has suffered much insult, even from the gentle Antonio. The pound of flesh which he demands in court is his legal right, by an agreement freely entered into with Antonio, and he is robbed of it not by any real legal process but by a trick of words which could hardly have any place in a fair system of justice. Shylock himself in this situation can scarcely believe that he is receiving fair treatment:

> Is that the law?

he asks, and Portia replies:

> Thyself shalt see the act. (IV.i.310)

– but she never shows it to him.

How, then, does Shakespeare bring out Shylock's essential wickedness? Firstly, perhaps, by making him an individual, not simply a representative of the Jewish nation. There is, in the play, practically nothing to suggest a hatred of Jews in general. Shylock understands the hatred in this way, but when he is insulted it is for what he himself is, not for what his race was by some supposed to be. As an individual he has turned against all Christians, and he chooses Antonio among them to be the one who will suffer most severely at his hands. The revenge he wants, as a man, to exact from all his enemies is gathered together in a hatred for one person, Antonio. Others are puzzled to know why he wants a piece of human flesh instead of money. He says, when he first appears in court:

> You'll ask me why I rather choose to have
> A weight of carrion flesh than to receive
> Three thousand ducats. (IV.i.40–2)

He gives no answer except to say that, as other people have fancies for things, he has a fancy for this. But we know differently; he has made an inhuman agreement which no one but Antonio, sad and tired of the world, would have accepted, and his aim in doing this is to get one Christian life as an object of his revenge. He hates deeply and passionately, and we are to hate him for it. So deep was Shylock's hatred that it would not be surprising to learn (and nothing in the play disagrees with this) that he was responsible for circulating the news of Antonio's losses at sea, and of exaggerating them; he might even have had news of them before he proposed his "merry bond", and have seen that he had every chance of getting Antonio into just the situation he longed for.

He is calculating and unkind; he makes cruel fun of Launce-lot's slips in the use of words:

Launcelot: . . . my young master doth expect your reproach [for *approach*].
Shylock: So do I his. (II.v.19–21)

and even family ties are secondary to his love of money; if the calculating business-man is uppermost in him when he appears before the court, the man beneath is perhaps most clearly seen through the eyes of others, of Salerio and Solanio, who tell how, with

> a passion so confused,
> So strange, outrageous, and so variable,
> . . . the dog Jew did utter in the streets:
> "My daughter! O my ducats! O my daughter!
> . . . Justice! find the girl!
> She hath the stones upon her, and the ducats!"
> (II.viii.12–15, 21–2)

All the boys of Venice laughed at him, but we must hate him for being so completely in the power of his evil desires.

To turn to *Portia* after this is to look at a sunnier world. When we first hear of her, in fact, we are led to believe that she shines with almost unearthly brightness:

> In Belmont is a lady richly left,
> And she is fair, and, fairer than that word,
> Of wondrous virtues. (I.i.160–2)

After this it comes as something of a relief to see, as we soon do, that she is really very human; for although she is rich in worldly goods, her dead father's will has ordered her to receive any suitors who come to woo her, and to make them submit to the lottery of the caskets; this makes her tired and unhappy. She has so far seen no one she likes except Bassanio. To other suitors as they come, to the Princes of Morocco and Arragon, she is cold and formal, and listens patiently to their long, self-important speeches, but to Bassanio, when he arrives at Belmont, she is warm and human. She begins by asking him to wait a day or two before making his choice, and in a moment wants him to delay for months. But he chooses quickly and, to her delight, correctly, so that without delay and with winning simplicity she accepts him as her husband:

> You see me, Lord Bassanio, where I stand,
> Such as I am . . .
>   an unlessoned girl, unschooled, unpractised;
> Happy in this, she is not yet so old
> But she may learn . . . (III.ii.149–50, 159–61)

She is so rich that the money Bassanio has borrowed for the voyage to Belmont seems nothing to her – she offers to pay the Jew twelve times as much. But when she hears Antonio's letter she knows that money will no longer be accepted; she therefore makes a plan to help Antonio, and only Nerissa is to know of it. Leaving her house in the hands of Lorenzo and Jessica, she goes with Nerissa to a place near Venice where, by arrangement with a cousin of hers who is a lawyer in Padua, she collects the robes of a lawyer, so that when we next see Nerissa she is dressed as a lawyer's clerk preparing the way for "a young and learned doctor" of law, who is, it is believed, waiting to enter the court in place of Bellario, the lawyer from Padua who is usually consulted. Portia's great moment has arrived: far from being a remote beauty, she handles the situation with brilliant self-assurance. When the bond seems clear and the penalty unavoidable, she appeals to Shylock, in a famous speech, to show mercy. He refuses, and so she leads him on to think that his case is won. She asks him to have a surgeon ready so that Antonio shall not bleed to death, but, since no such condition is mentioned on the bond, Shylock will not allow it. He praises her for her judgement, but she remains completely self-possessed, and asks if Antonio has anything to say. He speaks of his resignation to his fate, and then she must listen to Bassanio saying he would sacrifice all he has, including his wife, to stop Shylock from getting what was due to him. Portia (he is speaking to her about herself, of course, though he does not know it) makes a wonderfully plain, pointed remark:

> Your wife would give you little thanks for that
> If she were by to hear you make the offer.
>
> (IV.i.284–5)

Shakespeare liked making his heroines use such straightforward, unromantic language, and when they do they are at their most human and lovable.

But soon she is serious again and ready to turn the case against Shylock. By a trick she forces him to keep to the letter of the law as she says it is, and when this proves impossible she drives home her victory; Antonio is saved and Shylock ruined. Then Portia's wit comes into play again: as a reward for her work she asks Bassanio for his wedding ring (which in reality she had, of course, given him herself). He refuses, but later is persuaded by Antonio to send it after her. She hurries back to Belmont and arrives only a few moments before her husband, Bassanio, who is with Antonio. She acts as if she is meeting Antonio for the first time, and when the matter of the rings comes up she pretends to be very angry with her husband; but she soon turns to making fun of his apologies and gets Antonio to give Bassanio back his ring. And it is Portia, mistress of the play, who explains everything at last.

To know Portia is to admire and love her, for in one person she embodies the beauty and charm of a woman with the intelligence and quiet self-confidence of the best of men. We who are in the secret of her disguise see that in court she behaves like a man but without overstepping what is properly a woman's sphere. Yet she is never coldly brilliant, for in among her serious speeches are touches of humour and warm humanity which show that she is of this earth. To her suitors and her husband she is all that they could desire in a woman; to her servants she is admirable as an organizer; and when her great moment comes in the court she acts with a self-assurance which shows that she has no fears about the outcome of her efforts. Yet she does all this, and *is* all this, without show or pride, and that is probably Shakespeare's greatest achievement in his portrayal of her. In lesser hands she would have appeared too perfect, too remote from reality, too much the actor of a part. In the play she is none of these things; her spirit simply lightens whatever it touches.

Bassanio, it must be faced, is not her equal, and if love depended upon choosing equals they would never have married so happily. Early in the play he admits that he has already borrowed money in order to show off among his friends. And he is already in love with Portia. Antonio likes him very much and agrees to be held responsible for a further loan, which Bassanio gets, after some impatient discussion, from Shylock. At Belmont he is characteristically impatient to try his luck, despite Portia's wish that he should wait a little, but when he is confronted with the caskets he reasons well:

> So may the outward shows be least themselves;
> The world is still deceived with ornament.

He is not, therefore, attracted to the outward appearances of things, and to the lead he says:

> *Thy* paleness moves me more than eloquence.
> (III.ii.73-4, 106)

And so he chooses correctly and wins Portia. He is dizzy with his success, like an orator receiving praise from a great audience. But he must soon leave Belmont, for Antonio has sent him bad news, and Bassanio wants to be by his friend's side. When they are in court Bassanio flashes out in argument with Shylock until Antonio stops him, and he has to be satisfied with offering the money he has got from Portia. When all is well and the case is won he is persuaded to send his wedding-ring after Portia, not knowing it is she, but when she pretends to be shocked to know he has given it away he almost loses his head in shame. It is paralleled only by his surprise when he learns the truth.

Bassanio is, like Portia, lovable, but for a different reason: he is quick in action and not very thoughtful, a very human characteristic which people often find endearing. Friendships often go by opposites, and that would account for the patient, careful Antonio liking him so much. With him Bassanio is usually serious and his talk is full of imagery; but with others he is very ready to go beyond the truth and make things sound greater than they are. He is the sort of person who says in a difficult situation that he is willing to make great sacrifices but fails to do so when his words are put to the test. To Shylock's proposal of the bond he says:

> You shall not seal to such a bond for me;
> I 'll rather dwell in my necessity. (I.iii.148–9)

– which is less than the truth, because he puts up no further resistance to the arrangement. We have already seen how he says he would sacrifice everything, his life and all, to save Antonio. When he is caught without his wedding ring he says to himself:

> Why, I were best to cut my left hand off,
> And swear I lost the ring defending it. (v.i.176–7)

but we are not surprised to learn that nothing comes of it. It is a pleasant touch of humour when he tells Gratiano that he will not take him to Belmont unless he exercises a stricter control on what he says; for if he does not, Bassanio's chances of winning the lady may be worsened (II.ii.161ff.). We feel with Bassanio that his heart is in the right place and that age and experience, and life with Portia, will make him a fine man.

He is right, of course, in finding *Gratiano* "too wild, too rude, and bold of voice" to take with him when he wishes to appear in the best possible light. At first Gratiano is a contrast to Antonio, priding himself on being outspoken and casting suspicion on all quiet people as if they were silent only in order to appear wise. Antonio is not really comfortable with him and can talk only formally until he is gone. Gratiano promises to behave well at Belmont, but reserves the right to have one gay evening before they set out. There is to be a masque in the streets, during which Lorenzo plans to steal away with Jessica, and the masquers dress up for it at Gratiano's lodging. But before they can begin in earnest Antonio says the wind is up and Bassanio's ship is ready to sail at once.

The rest of Gratiano's story is quickly told. At Belmont he meets *Nerissa*, whom we have already seen talking pleasingly and discreetly with her mistress, Portia, about the suitors and the lottery of the caskets. He says to Bassanio:

> My eyes, my lord, can look as swift as yours:
> You saw the mistress, I beheld the maid;
> You loved, I loved . . . (III.ii.197–9)

and, when Bassanio is successful at the caskets, it is a foregone conclusion that Gratiano has won his Nerissa. Nerissa plays up well to Portia's scheme, and, when the time comes, carries her disguise faultlessly as a lawyer's clerk. In the court she remains cool and dutiful while Gratiano shouts angrily at Shylock, scolding him for his heartless cruelty. But he is silent when the trial begins in earnest until Shylock finds himself in a hopeless situation; then Gratiano turns Shylock's own phrases back at him:

> O learned judge!—Mark, Jew, a learned judge! (IV.i.313)

He, like Bassanio, is involved in trouble with a ring, for Nerissa gets hers from him just as Portia does from her husband. Nerissa says just the right things to bring out her mistress's pleasure as they see from afar the beauty of Belmont and the gardens at night, but she begins to quarrel with her husband as soon as he returns; it is over the ring, of course, and they both quickly laugh again when the secret is out.

They make a charming couple together; Gratiano's talkativeness and Nerissa's gay manner show them ideally suited to one another. They are both less influenced than most of the others by the customs of courtly formality; Nerissa is simple and direct in all she says, and Gratiano lets his tongue run on; both in their own ways, therefore, show their personalities without disguise. Here, then, is a second pair of happy lovers.

The third pair are the runaways *Jessica* and *Lorenzo*. They are lovers before the play begins, and Jessica is first seen as she gives a note to Launcelot Gobbo for Lorenzo, regretting that Gobbo is leaving her father's service for Bassanio's. But she too intends to leave her father's house soon, and looks to the time when Lorenzo will steal her away and marry her. He arranges this with the masquers, but something delays him and they are kept waiting. At last he is ready, and steals her away with some of Shylock's treasure that she throws down to him. Jessica is disguised for the journey in boy's clothes (in Shakespeare's day all the women's parts were played by boys, which made the disguising easier), and when we next see them they are in Belmont. Shakespeare manages the plot with such skill that even these lovers can fit easily into the main plan: while Portia is away in Venice, so as to appear secretly at court, Lorenzo and Jessica are left in charge of Belmont. They both greatly admire Portia and manage her household faithfully. They are the most responsive to the stillness of the night sky and the sweetness of the music in Belmont, and set the stage for Portia's return. They can exchange references to the classical stories of Greece and Rome without taking them altogether seriously:

Lorenzo: In such a night
        Did pretty Jessica, like a little shrew,
        Slander her love, and he forgave it her.
Jessica: I would out-night you did nobody come. (v.i.20–23)

They greet Portia, promise to keep the secret of her absence from Belmont, and, united in place and time with the two other pairs of happy lovers, are heard no more.

Lorenzo is, as far as we get to know him, good because he mixes with good people. Jessica, however bad her father and the home she comes from, is good and shows her goodness by bringing out the best in *Launcelot Gobbo*, the clown of the piece. At the beginning, Launcelot is Shylock's servant. He is not very clever nor very happy, but he aims his wit at big things, such as a debate with his conscience on the rightness of leaving Shylock's service. To our eyes the fun he makes of his father is rather cruel, but such fun was customary in the theatre of Shakespeare's time; it shows that he was a "merry devil" to have in Shylock's house, and Jessica liked to have him to talk to; even Shylock himself found him "kind enough". But he is the first to leave

Shylock, the beginning of Shylock's downfall, and he leaves him for a Christian. The way he and his father interrupt one another, mis-using words from time to time, when they ask Bassanio to employ Launcelot, is the best comedy in the play. Gobbo has no more to do except keep up his contact with Jessica (Lorenzo pretends this makes him jealous), and in the last scene to announce the return of Bassanio to Belmont.

6 *Some Suggestions for Further Reading*

Adams, J. C.: *The Globe Playhouse: its Design and Equipment*, Cambridge, U.S.A., 1942.

This book gives a detailed account of the theatre of Shakespeare's day.

Bradby, A.: *Shakespeare Criticism: 1919–1935*, Oxford, 1936.

A collection of modern pieces about Shakespeare's plays.

Granville-Barker, H.: *Prefaces to Shakespeare*, 4 volumes, London, 1923–1946.

Volume II has an essay on *The Merchant of Venice*. These prefaces are especially valuable as being written by an actor and producer for the theatre.

Granville-Barker, H., and Harrison, G. B. (editors): *A Companion to Shakespeare Studies*, Cambridge, 1934.

Jespersen, O.: *Growth and Structure of the English Language*, 9th edition, Oxford, 1958.

Chapter X of this book, "Shakespeare and the Language of Poetry", pays particular attention to Shylock.

Lamborn, E. A. G. and Harrison, G. B.: *Shakespeare: the Man and his Stage*, Oxford, 1923.

A short, well illustrated introduction to the subject.

Lee, S. and Onions, C. T. (editors): *Shakespeare's England: an Account of the Life and Manners of his Age*, 2 volumes, Oxford, 1916.

These are large books, and contain much detailed information from specialists on various aspects of the subject.

Onions, C. T.: *A Shakespeare Glossary*, Oxford, 1911.

Raleigh, W.: *Shakespeare*, London, 1907.

This is the oldest of the books mentioned here, but it is still probably the best general introduction to the subject.

Smith, D. Nichol: *Shakespeare Criticism: Heminge and Condell to Carlyle,* Oxford, 1916.
  A selection of older writings about Shakespeare.
Spurgeon, Caroline F. E.: *Shakespeare's Imagery and what it tells us,* Cambridge, 1935.
Wilson, F. P.: *Elizabethan and Jacobean,* Oxford, 1945.
  This tells of the period with special reference to literature.
Wilson, J. D.: *The Essential Shakespeare: a Biographical Adventure,* Cambridge, 1932.

Venice

DRAMATIS PERSONAE

THE DUKE OF VENICE
THE PRINCE OF MOROCCO ⎱ *suitors to Portia*
THE PRINCE OF ARRAGON ⎰
ANTONIO, *a merchant of Venice*
BASSANIO, *his friend, and a suitor to Portia*
GRATIANO ⎱
SALERIO ⎬ *friends of Antonio and Bassanio*
SOLANIO ⎰
LORENZO, *in love with Jessica*
SHYLOCK, *a Jew*
TUBAL, *a Jew, his friend*
LAUNCELOT GOBBO, *the clown of the play, Shylock's servant*
OLD GOBBO, *Launcelot's father*
LEONARDO, *Bassanio's servant*
BALTHAZAR ⎱ *Portia's servants*
STEPHANO ⎰

PORTIA, *an heiress, mistress of Belmont*
NERISSA, *her maid*
JESSICA, *Shylock's daughter*

RICH MERCHANTS OF VENICE, OFFICERS OF THE COURT
OF JUSTICE, A GAOLER, SERVANTS, AND OTHER
ATTENDANTS

The scenes are laid in Venice, and Portia's house at Belmont.

(I.i) Antonio, a merchant of Venice, tells his friends Salerio and Solanio that he is sad at heart but cannot say why. They suggest he is worried about his merchant-ships now at sea, but he denies this. He assures them he is not worried about love-affairs either. They can say only that he is sad because he is not merry. His friend Bassanio and two others come by. They, too, speak of Antonio's sadness, and at last Antonio and Bassanio are left together. With Bassanio, Antonio seems to be more at ease; they talk in a friendly way of Bassanio's love for the beautiful heiress Portia, and of how Antonio can help Bassanio with money so that he can go and seek her hand in marriage.

1 *In sooth* – "Truly, indeed".

2 *I am to learn* – "I have yet to find out".

3 *want-wit* – "fool".

4 *ado* – "trouble". Sadness makes him so foolish that he hardly recognizes himself.

5 *argosies* – "large merchant ships".

6 *portly* – "splendid", and also, perhaps, with the modern meaning of "with a large stomach", which might be a characteristic of the *rich burghers*, well fed and in heavy robes, mentioned in the next line.

7 *signiors* – "fine gentlemen". The word comes from the Italian *signor*.

8 *burghers* – "citizens".

9 *flood* – "seas".

10 *overpeer . . . to them* – "look down on (*overpeer*) the little (*petty*) trading boats (*traffickers*) that 'pay their respects' (*curtsy*) to them" (by bobbing up and down in the waves that the big ships make).

11 *had I such venture forth* – "if I had such a trading expedition (*venture*) at sea".

12 *affections* – "concerns".

13 *still* – "always".

14 *Plucking the grass . . . wind* – "picking up blades of grass and throwing them into the air to find out from which direction the wind was blowing".

15 *roads* – "seaways near to the shore where ships can anchor".

16 *out of doubt* – "undoubtedly".

THE MERCHANT OF VENICE

ACT ONE

Scene I. Venice. A street.

Enter ANTONIO, SALERIO, *and* SOLANIO

ANTONIO

In sooth,[1] I know not why I am so sad;
It wearies me; you say it wearies you;
But how I caught it, found it, or came by it,
What stuff 't is made of, whereof it is born,
I am to learn[2];   5
And such a want-wit[3] sadness makes of me
That I have much ado[4] to know myself.

SALERIO

Your mind is tossing on the ocean,
There where your argosies[5] with portly[6] sail,
Like signiors[7] and rich burghers[8] on the flood,[9]   10
Or as it were the pageants of the sea,
Do overpeer[10] the petty traffickers
That curtsy to them, do them reverence,
As they fly by them with their woven wings.

SOLANIO

Believe me, sir, had I such venture forth,[11]   15
The better part of my affections[12] would
Be with my hopes abroad. I should be still[13]
Plucking the grass[14] to know where sits the wind,
Peering in maps for ports, and piers, and roads;[15]
And every object that might make me fear   20
Misfortune to my ventures out of doubt[16]
Would make me sad.

I

17 *wind* – "breath".

18 *to an ague* – "into a fit of shivering". Even blowing on his soup to cool it would remind him of winds which might be threatening his ships.

19 *sandy hour-glass.* Before clocks were common, one way of telling the passing of time was to allow sand to fall in a thin stream from one glass bulb into another immediately below it. All the sand passed in a fixed time, e.g. one hour.

20 *my wealthy Andrew* – "my magnificent ship". A Spanish ship called the "St. Andrew" was captured by British sailors in 1596; this was very likely news when *The Merchant of Venice* was first performed. But it is possible that *Andrew* was used simply as a colourful name for a ship; sailors today sometimes refer to the British Navy as "the Andrew", though no one seems to know why. (See also Introduction, p. xiii.)

21 *Vailing . . . burial* – "lowering her high top sails below her ribs to kiss the ground where she will be buried". The image here is of the ship as a person, taking off his hat (the sails) in respect, lowering it to below his ribs (the main beams of the ship), and finally bowing low to kiss the ground (the sea).

22 *bethink me straight of* – "at once begin thinking about".

23 *Enrobe . . . silks.* The ship might be carrying rich silks which, if there was a shipwreck, would clothe (*Enrobe*) the stormy sea.

24 *but even now . . . nothing* – "at one moment worth all I have suggested and at the next moment worth nothing".

25 *bechanced* – "if it happened".

26 *in one bottom* – "in only one ship".

27 *Upon* – "dependent upon".

28 *Fie, fie!* – "Nonsense! Of course not!"

with portly sail [6]

2

SALERIO

My wind[17] cooling my broth
Would blow me to an ague[18] when I thought
What harm a wind too great might do at sea.
I should not see the sandy hour-glass[19] run   25
But I should think of shallows and of flats,
And see my wealthy Andrew[20] docked in sand,
Vailing[21] her high top lower than her ribs
To kiss her burial; should I go to church
And see the holy edifice of stone   30
And not bethink me straight of[22] dangerous rocks,
Which touching but my gentle vessel's side
Would scatter all her spices on the stream,
Enrobe[23] the roaring waters with my silks,
And, in a word, but even now[24] worth this,   35
And now worth nothing? Shall I have the thought
To think on this, and shall I lack the thought
That such a thing bechanced[25] would make me sad?
But tell not me, I know Antonio
Is sad to think upon his merchandise.   40

mover

ANTONIO

Believe me no, I thank my fortune for it –
My ventures are not in one bottom[26] trusted,   *denial.*
Nor to one place; nor is my whole estate
Upon[27] the fortune of this present year;
Therefore my merchandise makes me not sad.   45

SOLANIO

Why then, you are in love.

ANTONIO

Fie, fie![28]

3

29 *two-headed Janus.* Janus, a Roman god, was thought of as having two faces, which looked both ways; one face smiled, the other frowned.

30 *framed* – "made".

31 *evermore* – "continually".

32 *peep through their eyes* – "glance about them in fun, with their eyes half shut".

33 *parrots at a bagpiper:* parrots were thought to be stupid birds, who would laugh even at the solemn noise made by a bagpipe.

34 *other* – "others".

35 *vinegar aspect* – "sour look on the face".

36 *Nestor,* a legendary Greek hero famed for his wisdom and seriousness; if *he* recommended a joke, it must have been a good one.

37 *prevented me* – "come to do it for me".

38 *embrace th' occasion* – "take the opportunity".

39 *exceeding strange* – "very unfriendly".

40 *We 'll make . . . yours* – "Our free time shall be at your disposal."

the sandy hour-glass [19]

SOLANIO

Not in love neither; then let us say you are sad
Because you are not merry; and 't were as easy
For you to laugh and leap, and say you are merry
Because you are not sad. Now, by two-headed Janus,[29]   50
Nature hath framed[30] strange fellows in her time;
Some that will evermore[31] peep through their eyes,[32]
And laugh like parrots at a bagpiper;[33]
And other[34] of such vinegar aspect[35]
That they 'll not show their teeth in way of smile,   55
Though Nestor[36] swear the jest be laughable.

Enter BASSANIO, LORENZO, *and* GRATIANO

Here comes Bassanio, your most noble kinsman,
Gratiano, and Lorenzo. Fare ye well,
We leave you now with better company.

SALERIO

I would have stayed till I had made you merry,   60
If worthier friends had not prevented me.[37]

ANTONIO

Your worth is very dear in my regard.
I take it your own business calls on you,
And you embrace th' occasion[38] to depart.

SALERIO

Good morrow, my good lords.   65

BASSANIO

Good signiors both, when shall we laugh? say, when?
You grow exceeding strange;[39] must it be so?

SALERIO

We 'll make[40] our leisures to attend on yours.

[*Exeunt* SALERIO *and* SOLANIO

5

41 *You have ... world* – "You worry too much about life." Gratiano goes on talking even though Lorenzo has just wisely suggested that they should leave Antonio and Bassanio alone together.

42 *They lose it ... care* – "People who get the good things of this world with a great deal of worry lose the pleasure of them." This proverb is probably adapted from a verse of the Bible: "For whosoever will save his life shall lose it: and whosoever will lose his life for my sake shall find it" (*Matthew*, xvi.25).

43 *old wrinkles* – "the lines of age on the face".

44 *liver* and *heart* were taken as the organs of the body from which a man's character originated.

45 *his grandsire ... alabaster* – "(the monument of) his grandfather, cut in fine stone".

46 *creep into the jaundice* – "slowly get jaundice", an illness which makes one generally in low spirits.

47 *cream and mantle ... pond* – "go pale and become covered (as with a mask), like a pond in which the water is still".

48 *a wilful stillness entertain* – "keep silent on purpose".

49 *dressed in an opinion* – "given the reputation".

50 *conceit* – "understanding".

51 *As who should say* – "as much as to say".

A bagpipe [33]

LORENZO

My Lord Bassanio, since you have found Antonio,
We two will leave you, but at dinner-time   70
I pray you have in mind where we must meet.

BASSANIO

I will not fail you.

GRATIANO

You look not well, Signior Antonio,
You have[41] too much respect upon the world.
They lose it[42] that do buy it with much care –   75
Believe me, you are marvellously changed.

ANTONIO

I hold the world but as the world, Gratiano,
A stage, where every man must play a part,
And mine a sad one.

(least materialistic
"destiny")

GRATIANO

Let me play the fool;
With mirth and laughter let old wrinkles[43] come,   80
And let my liver rather heat with wine
Than my heart[44] cool with mortifying groans.
Why should a man whose blood is warm within
Sit like his grandsire,[45] cut in alabaster?
Sleep when he wakes? and creep into the jaundice[46]   85
By being peevish? I tell thee what, Antonio,
(I love thee, and 't is my love that speaks):
There are a sort of men whose visages
Do cream and mantle[47] like a standing pond,
And do a wilful stillness entertain,[48]   90
With purpose to be dressed in an opinion[49]
Of wisdom, gravity, profound conceit,[50]
As who should say,[51] "I am Sir Oracle,
And when I ope my lips, let no dog bark."
O my Antonio, I do know of these   95

7

52 *therefore only* – "for this reason only", i.e. keeping quiet.

53 *If they should ... fools* – "if they happen to say anything, those who hear them cannot avoid calling them fools, and will be damned for it". The Bible says: "whosoever shall say to his brother ... 'Thou fool', shall be in danger of hell fire" (*Matthew,* v.22).

54 *But fish not ... opinion* – "Do not use this sadness as a bait to catch a worthless fish (*fool gudgeon*), this reputation (for great cleverness)." The image here is taken from fishing: to use sadness and silence to obtain a reputation for wisdom is compared with fishing for a useless fish.

55 *moe* – "more".

56 *for this gear* – "at this rate, if this (discussion) continues".

57 *neat's tongue dried* – "an ox-tongue, dried and ready to eat".

58 *Is that anything now?* – "Is what he has just said of any value at all?"

59 *shall* – "have to".

cut in alabaster [45]

That therefore only[52] are reputed wise
For saying nothing; when I am very sure,
If they should[53] speak, would almost damn those ears
Which, hearing them, would call their brothers fools –
I 'll tell thee more of this another time.   100
But fish not[54] with this melancholy bait
For this fool gudgeon, this opinion.
Come, good Lorenzo, [*To the others*] – fare ye well a while,
I 'll end my exhortation after dinner.

LORENZO

Well, we will leave you then till dinner-time.   105
I must be one of these same dumb wise men,
For Gratiano never lets me speak.

GRATIANO

Well, keep me company but two years moe,[55]
Thou shalt not know the sound of thine own tongue.

ANTONIO

Fare you well; I 'll grow a talker for this gear.[56]   110

GRATIANO

Thanks i' faith, for silence is only commendable
In a neat's tongue dried,[57] and a maid not vendible.

[*Exeunt* GRATIANO *and* LORENZO

ANTONIO

Is that anything now?[58]

BASSANIO

Gratiano speaks an infinite deal of nothing – more than any
man in all Venice; his reasons are as two grains of wheat hid   115
in two bushels of chaff: you shall[59] seek all day ere you find
them, and when you have them, they are not worth the search.

9

60 *what lady is the same* – "who this lady is".

61 *disabled mine ... continuance* (line 124) – "reduced (*disabled*) my property (*estate*) by showing a somewhat (*something*) grander style of living (*swelling port*) than my small amount of money could keep up with".

62 *Nor do I ... rate* – "and I do not complain now at being reduced from such a grand style of living".

63 *gagged* – "bound".

64 *if it stand ... Within the eye of honour* – "if it is honourable, as you yourself always are"; *the eye* – "the sight".

65 *occasions* – "needs".

66 *shaft* – "arrow".

67 *his fellow ... flight* – "another (arrow) of the same power of flight".

68 *with more adviséd watch* – "watching it more carefully".

69 *childhood proof* – "instance from childhood".

70 *what follows ... innocence* – "what I am now going to do (viz. ask you to lend me more money) is completely honourable". The *innocence* is free from moral fault, like a child's; he therefore urges the *childhood proof.*

ANTONIO

Well, tell me now what lady is the same[60]
To whom you swore a secret pilgrimage,
That you to-day promised to tell me of.   120

BASSANIO

'T is not unknown to you, Antonio,
How much I have disabled [61] mine estate
By something showing a more swelling port
Than my faint means would grant continuance;
Nor do I[62] now make moan to be abridged
From such a noble rate, but my chief care   125
Is to come fairly off from the great debts
Wherein my time, something too prodigal,
Hath left me gagged.[63] To you Antonio
I owe the most in money and in love,
And from your love I have a warranty   130
To unburden all my plots and purposes
How to get clear of all the debts I owe.

ANTONIO

I pray you, good Bassanio, let me know it,
And if it stand,[64] as you yourself still do,
Within the eye of honour, be assured   135
My purse, my person, my extremest means
Lie all unlocked to your occasions.[65]

BASSANIO

In my school-days, when I had lost one shaft,[66]
I shot his fellow[67] of the self-same flight
The self-same way, with more advised watch,[68]   140
To find the other forth, and by adventuring both,
I oft found both; I urge this childhood proof[69]
Because what follows[70] is pure innocence.
I owe you much, and, like a wilful youth,   145

11

71 *self* – "same".

72 *or* – "either".

73 *your latter hazard* – "the second loan you have risked".

74 *rest* – "remain".

75 *herein spend but time* – "in this you are just wasting time".

76 *To wind . . . with circumstance* – "to talk . . . in an indirect, complicated way".

77 *making question of my uttermost* – "questioning whether I would do everything I could (*my uttermost*) for you".

78 *prest unto it* – "ready to do it".

79 *richly left* – rich in property left her by her family.

80 *nothing undervalued To* – "in no way lower in worth than . . .". The other Portia mentioned here was the wife of Brutus, one of Julius Caesar's murderers. (Her name is usually spelt Porcia.)

81 *a golden fleece . . . quest of her* (line 171). In a classical story, Jason, a Greek hero, won back a kingdom which was his right by obtaining a golden fleece belonging to the King of Colchis and guarded by an ever-watchful dragon. Portia's golden hair, and her golden riches, make her house (*seat*) at Belmont like the beach of Colchis (*Colchos*' *strand*), for many adventurers come to win her.

82 *I have . . . thrift* – "my thoughts foresee such good success (in this venture)". There is going to be a lottery for Portia's hand, but Bassanio does not yet know of it.

That which I owe is lost, but if you please
To shoot another arrow that self[71] way
Which you did shoot the first, I do not doubt,
As I will watch the aim, or[72] to find both,
Or bring your latter hazard[73] back again,   150
And thankfully rest[74] debtor for the first.

ANTONIO

You know me well, and herein spend but time[75]
To wind[76] about my love with circumstance,
And out of doubt you do me now more wrong
In making question of my uttermost[77]   155
Than if you had made waste of all I have.
Then do but say to me what I should do
That in your knowledge may by me be done,
And I am prest unto it:[78] therefore speak.

BASSANIO

In Belmont is a lady richly left,[79]   160
And she is fair, and, fairer than that word,
Of wondrous virtues. Sometimes from her eyes
I did receive fair speechless messages.
Her name is Portia, nothing undervalued
To[80] Cato's daughter, Brutus' Portia,   165
Nor is the wide world ignorant of her worth,
For the four winds blow in from every coast
Renownéd suitors, and her sunny locks
Hang on her temples like a golden fleece,[81]
Which makes her seat of Belmont Colchos' strand,   170
And many Jasons come in quest of her.
O my Antonio, had I but the means
To hold a rival place with one of them,
I have[82] a mind presages me such thrift
That I should questionless be fortunate.   175

ANTONIO

Thou know'st that all my fortunes are at sea,

13

83 *commodity* – "merchandise".

84 *a present sum* – "ready money".

85 *Try what ... Venice do* – "find out how much money you can borrow in Venice by giving my name as security".

86 *racked* – "stretched".

87 *of my trust ... sake* – (perhaps) "on my credit or simply taking it instead of me".

(I.ii) Portia and her maid Nerissa are seen discussing the method which Portia's father has willed for her to find a husband: her suitors must each choose one of three caskets, made of gold, silver, and lead, and the winning casket has Portia's picture inside. The women talk about the suitors who have so far come to Belmont from distant countries; Portia is not attracted to any of them, and is glad to know that none is willing to submit to the luck of the caskets. But they remember with pleasure the visit of Bassanio. The arrival of yet another suitor, the Prince of Morocco, is then announced.

1 *no mean happiness ... mean* – "a great happiness, therefore, to be placed in moderate circumstances" (i.e. not too rich and not too poor). The less noble characters in Shakespeare's plays very often play with words as Nerissa plays with *mean* in this passage.

2 *superfluity ... white hairs* – "a person who overdoes or has too much of everything gets white hairs sooner" (i.e. he ages more quickly).

3 *sentences* – "principles".

4 *pronounced* – "spoken".

5 *had been* – "would have been".

Neither have I money, nor commodity[83]
To raise a present sum;[84] therefore go forth;
Try what[85] my credit can in Venice do,
That shall be racked[86] even to the uttermost   180
To furnish thee to Belmont to fair Portia.
Go, presently inquire, and so will I,
Where money is; and I no question make
To have it of my trust,[87] or for my sake.   [*Exeunt*

Scene II. Belmont. *A room in Portia's house.*

Enter PORTIA *with her waiting-woman* NERISSA.

PORTIA

By my troth, Nerissa, my little body is aweary of this great
world.

NERISSA

You would be, sweet madam, if your miseries were in the
same abundance as your good fortunes are; and yet for aught
I see, they are as sick that surfeit with too much, as they that   5
starve with nothing; it is no mean happiness[1] therefore to be
seated in the mean – superfluity[2] comes sooner by white
hairs, but competency lives longer.

PORTIA

Good sentences,[3] and well pronounced.[4]

NERISSA

They would be better if well followed.   10

PORTIA

If to do were as easy as to know what were good to do, chapels
had been[5] churches, and poor men's cottages princes' palaces.
It is a good divine that follows his own instructions. I can easier
teach twenty what were good to be done than be one of the

6 *the blood.* It was thought that passionate feelings came from the blood. A *hot temper* from the blood, therefore, is contrasted with a *cold decree* from the brain.

7 *such a hare ... cripple* – "youthful high spirits are like the hare, which jumps over the nets (*meshes*) of slow-moving (*cripple*) good advice". A long explanation such as this unavoidably slows down the speed and neatness of Shakespeare's images; for him *meshes* continues the image of *hare*, *madness* is contrasted with *good counsel* and *the youth* with *the cripple*, all in a very few words.

8 *in the fashion* – "the right way".

9 *O me* – "Ah!", said with a sigh.

10 *will ... will.* Portia plays on these words: the first means "wish", the second "directions as to what is to happen to someone's property when he dies". The arrangement of the lottery by which a husband is to be found for Portia is an important part of the plot, and Shakespeare explains it most effectively by making Portia mention it first, but giving Nerissa, who is not directly concerned, the lines which describe it in detail. She can then ask Portia (ll. 29–30) how matters stand at the moment.

11 *over-name them* – "read the whole list of them".

12 *level* – "guess".

13 *Neapolitan* – "of Naples (in Italy)".

14 *colt*, a young horse, and so a wild young man.

15 *parts* – "qualities".

16 *afeared* – "afraid".

17 *County Palatine*: a powerful lord whose authority was as complete as the King's over a certain part of the country.

PORTIA

16

twenty to follow mine own teaching; the brain may devise 15
laws for the blood,[6] but a hot temper leaps o'er a cold decree;
– such a hare[7] is madness the youth, to skip o'er the meshes of
good counsel the cripple. But this reasoning is not in the
fashion[8] to choose me a husband. – O me,[9] the word "choose"!
I may neither choose who I would, nor refuse who I dislike, so 20
is the will[10] of a living daughter curbed by the will of a dead
father. Is it not hard, Nerissa, that I cannot choose one, nor refuse
none?

NERISSA

Your father was ever virtuous, and holy men at their death
have good inspirations; therefore the lottery that he hath 25
devised in these three chests, of gold, silver, and lead, whereof
who chooses his meaning chooses you, will no doubt never
be chosen by any rightly, but one who you shall rightly love.
But what warmth is there in your affection towards any of
these princely suitors that are already come? 30

PORTIA

I pray thee over-name them,[11] and as thou namest them, I will
describe them. And according to my description level[12] at
my affection.

NERISSA

First there is the Neapolitan[13] prince.

PORTIA

Ay, that's a colt[14] indeed, for he doth nothing but talk of his 35
horse, and he makes it a great appropriation to his own good
parts[15] that he can shoe him himself. I am much afeared[16] my
lady his mother played false with a smith.

NERISSA

Then is there the County Palatine.[17]

18 *as who should say* – "as much as to say".

19 *choose* – "do as you choose; have it your own way".

20 *prove the weeping philosopher* – "become 'the weeping philosopher'", i.e. Heraclitus of Ephesus, who regretted so deeply the stupidity of mankind that he withdrew from the world and lived alone in the mountains.

21 *a death's head . . . mouth* – "a skull and cross-bones", as are sometimes cut in stone on a tomb to represent death.

22 *How say you by* – "What do you think of".

23 *falls straight a-capering* – "at once begins jumping about (to the music)".

24 *What say you then to Falconbridge?* – "What do you think of Falconbridge, then?" But Portia purposely misunderstands her, so as to make a joke of the Englishman's inability to speak foreign languages – we are to suppose that they are all talking Italian. She tells how she says "nothing to him" because he cannot understand her.

25 *come into . . . swear* – "bear witness to the fact".

26 *a poor . . . English* – "very little English indeed".

27 *a proper man's picture* – "a fine (*proper*) man in appearance".

28 *a dumb-show*, a part of a play which was presented without words.

29 *suited* – "dressed".

30 *doublet . . . round hose* – the thick outer coat and tight-fitting trousers worn by men in Shakespeare's day. The Englishman of the time had a reputation for taking his styles of clothing from many countries.

Doublet and hose [30]

18

PORTIA

He doth nothing but frown, as who should say,[18] "an you will   40
not have me, choose".[19] He hears merry tales and smiles not;
I fear he will prove the weeping philosopher[20] when he grows
old, being so full of unmannerly sadness in his youth. I had
rather be married to a death's-head[21] with a bone in his
mouth, than to either of these. God defend me from these   45
two.

NERISSA

How say you by[22] the French lord, Monsieur Le Bon?

PORTIA

God made him, and therefore let him pass for a man. In truth
I know it is a sin to be a mocker, but he! why he hath a horse
better than the Neapolitan's, a better bad habit of frowning than   50
the Count Palatine; he is every man in no man; if a throstle
sing, he falls straight a-capering.[23] He will fence with his own
shadow. If I should marry him, I should marry twenty
husbands. If he would despise me, I would forgive him, for
if he love me to madness, I shall never requite him.   55

NERISSA

What say you then to Falconbridge,[24] the young baron of
England?

PORTIA

You know I say nothing to him, for he understands not me,   contemporary)
nor I him; he hath neither Latin, French, nor Italian, and you
will come into[25] the court and swear that I have a poor[26]   60
pennyworth in the English. He is a proper man's picture,[27]
but alas! who can converse with a dumb-show?[28] How oddly
he is suited![29] I think he bought his doublet in Italy, his round
hose[30] in France, his bonnet in Germany, and his behaviour
everywhere.   65

NERISSA

What think you of the Scottish lord, his neighbour?

31 *borrowed . . . ear of* – "had a blow on the head from".

32 *again* – "back".

33 *the Frenchman . . . another* – "the Frenchman solemnly promised to give the Englishman another such blow". This is legal language used as a joke in connection with fighting. A person who borrowed money made a bond, or written agreement, to pay it back at a certain time, and sealed it as a sign of his consent. (See, for example, Antonio's words at I.iii.146: *Content, in faith; I'll seal to such a bond.*) Another person (*his surety*), who made himself responsible for seeing that the agreement was carried out, put his seal underneath (*sealed under*). In Shakespeare's day the Scots and the French were often united against the English; here again, therefore, Shakespeare jokingly brings out national characteristics in the persons of the suitors.

34 *best* and *beast* (in the next line but one) were probably pronounced alike in Shakespeare's day, making this sentence yet another example of Portia's word-play.

35 *fall* – "happens".

36 *make shift* – "manage".

37 *should* – "would (unavoidably)".

38 *Rhenish*: of the district of R. Rhine.

39 *contrary* – "wrong". Something inside the "right" casket will show that the man who chooses it will become Portia's husband.

40 *is* for *are*.

41 *by some other sort* – "in some other way", with a joke on an old use of *sort* to mean "lottery".

PORTIA

That he hath a neighbourly charity in him, for he borrowed[31]
a box of the ear of the Englishman, and swore he would pay
him again[32] when he was able. I think the Frenchman[33] became
his surety, and sealed under for another.   70

NERISSA

How like you the young German, the Duke of Saxony's
nephew?

PORTIA

Very vilely in the morning when he is sober, and most vilely
in the afternoon when he is drunk; when he is best,[34] he is a
little worse than a man, and when he is worst he is little   75
better than a beast. An the worst fall[35] that ever fell, I hope I
shall make shift[36] to go without him.

NERISSA

If he should offer to choose, and choose the right casket, you
should[37] refuse to perform your father's will, if you should
refuse to accept him.   80

PORTIA

Therefore, for fear of the worst, I pray thee set a deep glass of
Rhenish[38] wine on the contrary[39] casket, for if the devil be
within, and that temptation without, I know he will choose
it. I will do anything, Nerissa, ere I will be married to a
sponge.   85

NERISSA

You need not fear, lady, the having any of these lords; they
have acquainted me with their determinations, which is,[40]
indeed, to return to their home, and to trouble you with no
more suit, unless you may be won by some other sort[41] than
your father's imposition, depending on the caskets.   90

42 *Sibylla*, a prophetess, here the Sibyl of Cumae, who, according to a classical story, was told by Apollo that he would grant her any request she would like to make. She chose to ask that she might live for as many years as there were grains of sand in her hand.

43 *Diana*, the virgin goddess.

44 *parcel* – "set".

45 *Venetian* – "a person from Venice".

46 *four*: six have, in fact, been mentioned, and to call them four is perhaps Shakespeare's own slip. It makes possible the word-play with *forerunner* in the following line.

47 *condition* – "character".

PORTIA

If I live to be as old as Sibylla,[42] I will die as chaste as Diana,[43]
unless I be obtained by the manner of my father's will. I am
glad this parcel[44] of wooers are so reasonable, for there is not
one among them but I dote on his very absence; and I pray
God grant them a fair departure.   95

NERISSA

Do you not remember, lady, in your father's time, a Venetian,[45]
a scholar and a soldier, that came hither in company of the
Marquis of Montferrat?

PORTIA

Yes, yes, it was Bassanio, as I think so was he called.

NERISSA

True, madam, he of all the men that ever my foolish eyes 100
looked upon was the best deserving a fair lady.

PORTIA

I remember him well, and I remember him worthy of thy
praise.
Enter a Serving-man.
How now, what news?

SERVING-MAN

The four[46] strangers seek for you, madam, to take their 105
leave; and there is a forerunner come from a fifth, the Prince
of Morocco, who brings word the prince his master will be
here to-night.

PORTIA

If I could bid the fifth welcome with so good heart as I can
bid the other four farewell, I should be glad of his approach; 110
if he have the condition[47] of a saint and the complexion of a
devil, I had rather he should shrive me than wive me.

48 *Sirrah, go before* – "You (to the serving-man), go in front of us". As often in Shakespeare's plays, the scene ends with two rhyming lines, *before, door*.

49 *Whiles*–"Whilst"

(1.iii) Bassanio has already begun to discuss business with Shylock. He wants to borrow 3,000 ducats, for three months, in the name of his friend Antonio. Shylock tells how he believes Antonio's name is a good security, even though his fortune is largely in ships at sea. But he also reflects that he hates Antonio because Antonio lends money without charging interest, which is bad for business, and because Antonio has ill-treated him. When Antonio himself comes up to them, an agreement is soon made; Shylock will lend the money, but if it is not repaid within three months, Antonio must give a pound of his flesh to Shylock.

1 *ducats*, Italian coins; four ducats were worth about one pound sterling.

2 *well*, said with rising pitch in the voice; Shylock is thinking over each point of the proposal.

3 *May you stead me?* – "Can you help me?" Bassanio is obviously in a hurry, and does not wait for an answer.

Come, Nerissa. [*To the Serving-man.*] Sirrah, go before.[48]
Whiles[49] we shut the gate upon one wooer, another knocks
at the door.   *Complet. to finish off* [*Exeunt* 115

Scene III. Venice. A street

Enter BASSANIO *with* SHYLOCK *the Jew.*

SHYLOCK   *— cagey, weary*

Three thousand ducats,[1] well.

BASSANIO   *— impatient*

Ay sir, for three months.

SHYLOCK

For three months, – well.[2]

BASSANIO

For the which, as I told you, Antonio shall be bound.

SHYLOCK

Antonio shall become bound, – well.   5

BASSANIO

May you stead me?[3] Will you pleasure me? Shall I know your
answer?

SHYLOCK

Three thousand ducats for three months, and Antonio bound.

BASSANIO

Your answer to that?

SHYLOCK   *good = good for money.*

Antonio is a good man.   10

BASSANIO

Have you heard any imputation to the contrary?

good $\frac{=}{25}$ not being bad

4 *sufficient* – "sufficiently rich", and therefore a good security.

5 *are in supposition* – "have to be taken on trust", since his property is all outside Venice, and will become available only in the future.

6 *argosy*, large merchant ship.

7 *upon the Rialto* – "at the Exchange of Venice", where business was done.

8 *squandered* – (perhaps) "scattered foolishly".

9 *Be assured* . . . This exchange of words is at the same time realistic and carefully balanced and pointed. Shylock says, "I think . . ."; Bassanio, now very impatient to reach an agreement, says, "Be assured. . .", i.e. "I am telling you for certain". Shylock, fearing that he is urged to act before taking proper thought, says, "I *will* be assured . . .", and then plays on the word *assured*, making it now mean "with security" in the commercial sense. After that he goes back to thinking before agreeing: "I will bethink me".

10 *pork*. Being a strict Jew, Shylock would not eat the meat of the pig.

11 *your prophet the Nazarite*, Jesus of Nazareth, Christ. Jesus once commanded evil spirits to come out of two men and enter a herd of pigs; the pigs ran into a lake and were drowned. For this reason, Shylock calls pigs the habitation of the devil. (*Matthew*, viii. 28–34, etc.)

12 *fawning publican*. This phrase is probably another memory of the Bible; there, publicans are the hated Jewish tax-collectors who worked for Rome against their own people. Such men would not be used to *fawning*, and neither would the rich Antonio, but here he now comes looking like someone hateful to the Jews and wanting to borrow money.

13 *for* – "because".

upon the Rialto [7]

SHYLOCK

Ho no, no, no, no; my meaning in saying he is a good man
is to have you understand me that he is sufficient[4]. Yet his
means are in supposition;[5] he hath an argosy[6] bound to Tripolis,
another to the Indies. I understand, moreover, upon the   15
Rialto,[7] he hath a third at Mexico, a fourth for England, and
other ventures he hath squandered[8] abroad. But ships are but
boards, sailors but men; there be land-rats and water-rats,
water-thieves, and land-thieves, (I mean pirates), and then
there is the peril of waters, winds, and rocks; the man is,   20
notwithstanding, sufficient, – three thousand ducats, – I think
I may take his bond.

BASSANIO

Be assured[9] you may.

SHYLOCK

I *will* be assured I may: and, that I may be assured, I will
bethink me. May I speak with Antonio?   25

BASSANIO

If it please you to dine with us.

SHYLOCK

Yes, to smell pork,[10] to eat of the habitation which your
prophet the Nazarite[11] conjured the devil into. I will buy with
you, sell with you, talk with you, walk with you, and so
following, but I will not eat with you, drink with you, nor   30
pray with you. What news on the Rialto? – Who is he comes
here?

Enter ANTONIO

BASSANIO

This is Signior Antonio.

SHYLOCK [*Aside*]

How like a fawning publican[12] he looks!
I hate him for[13] he is a Christian: 35

27

14 *low simplicity* – "humble foolishness".

15 *the rate of usance.* In Shakespeare's day, and for many centuries before, Jews played a leading part in the business of money-lending. They lent money to people and charged them interest *(usury, usance)* on the loan, and the popular view was that no Christian could do this because it implied getting money without working for it, whereas the Christian religion taught that to get bread to eat one must work for money to buy it. In the play, *usance* and *usury* mean "interest", not, as in Modern English, the charging of too high a rate of interest; lending on interest was still considered wicked, for the reason stated. Antonio, the Christian, refuses to do it – "He lends out money gratis" – and so the rate of interest earned by loans in the market is reduced.

16 *upon the hip* – "at a disadvantage". The image is taken from wrestling, a sport in which two men struggle to throw each other to the ground. To have a man 'on the hip' in this sport is to hold him in a position from which he can be thrown down.

17 *thrift*, another, more agreeable, word for *interest* or *usury*.

18 *debating . . . store* – "thinking about how much money I have at the moment".

19 *the gross* – "the full amount".

20 *furnish me* – "provide me (with it)".

21 *soft!* – "be quiet (so that I can think further)".

22 *Rest you fair* – "(May God give you) good health in the future!"

23 *Your worship . . . mouths* – "you, noble sir, were the man we last mentioned"; i.e. "we have just been talking about you".

24 *albeit* – "although".

25 *excess* – "interest" on a money loan.

26 *ripe* – "urgent".

27 *Is he . . . would?* – "Does he already know how much you want?"

But more, for that in low simplicity[14]
He lends out money gratis, and brings down
The rate of usance[15] here with us in Venice.
If I can catch him once upon the hip,[16]
I will feed fat the ancient grudge I bear him.   40
He hates our sacred nation, and he rails,
Even there where merchants most do congregate,
On me, my bargains, and my well-won thrift,[17]
Which he calls interest; cursed be my tribe
If I forgive him!

BASSANIO

Shylock, do you hear?

SHYLOCK

I am debating[18] of my present store,
And by the near guess of my memory
I cannot instantly raise up the gross[19]
Of full three thousand ducats: what of that?
Tubal, a wealthy Hebrew of my tribe,   50
Will furnish me;[20] but soft![21] how many months
Do you desire? [To ANTONIO]. Rest you fair,[22] good signior;
Your worship[23] was the last man in our mouths.

ANTONIO

Shylock, albeit[24] I neither lend nor borrow
By taking nor by giving of excess,[25]   55
Yet to supply the ripe[26] wants of my friend,
I'll break a custom. [To BASSANIO]. Is he[27] yet possessed
How much ye would?

SHYLOCK

Ay, ay, three thousand ducats.

ANTONIO

And for three months.

28 *I had forgot.* Shylock had not in fact forgotten, but this repetition of the suggested conditions of the loan gives him further time to think about it; and it would be bad business to appear too eager.

29 *Me thoughts* – "I thought"; this old form originally meant "It seemed to me".

30 *When Jacob grazed* . . . In the passage that follows, Shylock recalls the story of Jacob and Laban, as told in the Bible (*Genesis,* xxx. 25–43). Jacob looked after his uncle Laban's sheep for many years, but would take no wages in return. Instead he asked to have all the lambs which were not pure white. Laban agreed, but deceived Jacob by taking away the sheep which were not pure white. Nevertheless, Jacob believed that if black and white striped sticks were set up among the stronger sheep when they were breeding, they bore lambs which were not pure white; and these were his. The weaker sheep did not breed among the sticks, and their lambs were Laban's. Shylock tells this story, apparently, to show that where business is concerned, sentimental considerations of friendship and kinship should not intrude. By telling it he annoys Antonio, who is already impatient to have an answer to his request; and Shylock is also obviously proud of the business sense of Jacob his ancestor – "This was a way to thrive, and he was blest" (line 82, below).

31 *This Jacob . . . third . . .* Jacob's father was Isaac, Isaac's father was Abraham (*Abram*); in this sense Jacob was the *third possessor* of Abraham's property. Jacob's *wise mother* managed things to his advantage (*wrought in his behalf*) by making him trick his elder brother, Esau, and deceive his father into giving him all his property when Isaac died.

32 *were compromised* – "had agreed on terms".

33 *eanlings* – "newborn lambs".

34 *fall as Jacob's hire* – "become Jacob's reward for his services".

35 *rank* – "ready".

36 *pilled* – "stripped (of bark)". Here *me* has no separate meaning.

37 *the deed of kind* – "act of breeding".

38 *fulsome* – "strong".

39 *eaning time* – "lambing season".

40 *fall parti-coloured lambs* – "give birth to lambs which were partly white and partly black".

SHYLOCK

I had forgot[28] – three months; [*To* BASSANIO] you told me
  so.   60
Well then, your bond; and let me see – but hear you,
Me thoughts[29] you said you neither lend nor borrow
Upon advantage.

ANTONIO

I do never use it.

SHYLOCK

When Jacob grazed[30] his uncle Laban's sheep –
This Jacob[31] from our holy Abram was   65
(As his wise mother wrought in his behalf)
The third possessor; ay, he was the third . . .

ANTONIO

And what of him? did *he* take interest?

SHYLOCK

No, not take interest, not as you would say
Directly interest; mark what Jacob did: 70
When Laban and himself were compromised[32]
That all the eanlings[33] which were streaked and pied
Should fall as Jacob's hire,[34] the ewes being rank[35]
In end of autumn turnéd to the rams,
And when the work of generation was   75
Between these woolly breeders in the act,
The skilful shepherd pilled[36] me certain wands,
And in the doing of the deed of kind[37]
He stuck them up before the fulsome[38] ewes,
Who, then conceiving, did in eaning time[39]   80
Fall parti-coloured lambs,[40] and those were Jacob's.
This was a way to thrive, and he was blest;
And thrift is blessing if men steal it not.

41 *served for* – "was an agent for"; i.e. God worked through him, for otherwise what he did, being sinful, would not have brought him glory.

42 *Was this . . . good?* – "Was this brought into the conversation to prove that it is good to take interest (on loans of money)?"

43 *breed . . .* It was an old idea that to make money "breed" more money was sinful.

44 *the rate*, i.e. the rate of interest. Shylock is working it out on the basis of the *annual* rate; he therefore talks of three months in relation to twelve months.

45 *beholding*; another form of *beholden* – "bound by debt".

46 *rated* – "scolded angrily".

47 *sufferance* – "suffering without complaint".

48 *badge* – "distinguishing mark".

49 *gaberdine*, a long, loose outer garment; it may have been the conventional dress of a Jew on the English stage of Shakespeare's day.

my Jewish gaberdine [49]

ANTONIO

This was a venture, sir, that Jacob served for,[41]
A thing not in his power to bring to pass,   85
But swayed and fashioned by the hand of heaven.
Was this[42] inserted to make interest good?
Or is your gold and silver ewes and rams?

SHYLOCK

I cannot tell, I make it breed[43] as fast –
But note me, signior . . .

Justifying usury

ANTONIO

              Mark you this, Bassanio,   90
The devil can cite Scripture for his purpose;
An evil soul producing holy witness
Is like a villain with a smiling cheek,
A goodly apple rotten at the heart.
O what a goodly outside falsehood hath!   95

especially so in Old Testament

SHYLOCK

Three thousand ducats, 't is a good round sum.
Three months from twelve—then let me see the rate.[44]

ANTONIO

Well, Shylock, shall we be beholding[45] to you?

SHYLOCK

Signior Antonio, many a time and oft
In the Rialto you have rated[46] me   100
About my moneys and my usances.
Still have I borne it with a patient shrug,
For sufferance[47] is the badge[48] of all our tribe.
You call me misbeliever, cut-throat dog,
And spit upon my Jewish gaberdine,[49]   105
And all for use of that which is mine own.
Well then, it now appears you need my help.

Christian's wrong.

50 *Go to, then,* a remark showing annoyance and impatience: "And now look!" is a modern phrase with a similar meaning.

51 *void your rheum* – "spit".

52 *moneys is your suit* – "your request is for sums of money".

53 *in a bondman's key* – "in a servant's tone of voice".

54 *like* – "likely".

55 *when did . . . friend?* – "when did a friend take interest for money he lent to a friend?" As in line 89 above, the image is of money not being like an animal which can "breed" profitably; between friends, at least, it must be *barren*, i.e. *not* able to breed.

56 *break* – "go bankrupt".

57 *doit,* a very small sum of money.

58 *kind* – "generous" and also "according to nature", i.e. what Shylock has to propose is good and worthy of friendship.

34

Go to, then,[50] you come to me, and you say,
"Shylock, we would have moneys"; *you* say so;
You that did void your rheum[51] upon my beard, 110
And foot me as you spurn a stranger cur
Over your threshold; moneys is your suit.[52]
What should I say to you? Should I not say:
"Hath a dog money? Is it possible
A cur can lend three thousand ducats?"; or 115
Shall I bend low, and in a bondman's key,[53]
With bated breath and whispering humbleness
Say this:
"Fair sir, you spat on me on Wednesday last;
You spurned me such a day; another time 120
You called me dog; and for these courtesies
I 'll lend you thus much moneys"?

ANTONIO

I am as like[54] to call thee so again,
To spit on thee again, to spurn thee too.
If thou wilt lend this money, lend it not 125
As to thy friends, for when did[55] friendship take
A breed for barren metal of his friend?
But lend it rather to thine enemy,
Who if he break,[56] thou may'st with better face
Exact the penalty. 130

SHYLOCK

Why, look you, how you storm!
I would be friends with you, and have your love,
Forget the shames that you have stained me with,
Supply your present wants, and take no doit[57]
Of usance for my moneys, and you 'll not hear me – 135
This is kind[58] I offer.

BASSANIO

This were kindness.

35

59 *single bond;* he probably means a bond without any conditions to it; but perhaps it is to be one with only Antonio's seal to it, which would mean that Shylock accepted it out of "kindness" without the names of sureties, people who agreed to be bound on Antonio's behalf.

60 *nominated for* – "named as".

61 *dwell* – "remain".

62 *teaches them suspect* – "teach them to suspect".

63 *profitable neither* – "nor profitable".

64 *muttons, beefs* – "sheep, cows".

SHYLOCK

This kindness will I show.
Go with me to a notary; seal me there
Your single bond,[59] and, in a merry sport,
If you repay me not on such a day,   140
In such a place, such sum or sums as are
Expressed in the condition, let the forfeit
Be nominated for[60] an equal pound
Of your fair flesh, to be cut off and taken
In what part of your body pleaseth me.   145

ANTONIO

Content, in faith; I 'll seal to such a bond,
And say there is much kindness in the Jew.

BASSANIO

You shall not seal to such a bond for me;
I 'll rather dwell[61] in my necessity.

ANTONIO

Why, fear not, man, I will not forfeit it –   150
Within these two months, that 's a month before
This bond expires, I do expect return
Of thrice three times the value of this bond.

SHYLOCK

O father Abram, what these Christians are,
Whose own hard dealings teaches them suspect[62]   155
The thoughts of others! Pray you, tell me this:
If he should break his day, what should I gain
By the exaction of the forfeiture?
A pound of man's flesh taken from a man
Is not so estimable, profitable neither,[63]   160
As flesh of muttons, beefs,[64] or goats. I say,
To buy his favour I extend this friendship;

37

65 *adieu* – "farewell".

66 *purse the ducats straight* – "put the ducats into my purse at once".

67 *fearful* – "causing fear" (in Shylock), because the servant cannot be trusted; and so "untrustworthy". In the next line Shylock calls this servant *an unthrifty knave*, and unthriftiness is just what Shylock cannot endure. He leaves, having persuaded Antonio that the bond is little more than a joke, since on Antonio's side the loan is only a small fraction of his fortune, and on Shylock's the forfeit, if it is not repaid, is possibly cruel to the borrower but quite worthless to him himself. It therefore seems that the agreement need not be taken seriously, especially because after Antonio had mentioned a penalty (line 130) Shylock's attitude changed, and he now talks of kindness and friendship.

68 *Hie thee* – "Hurry away".

69 *I like not ...* This line sums up much of the action of the scene, and the powerful effect of what it states is partly due to the balance of its words: *fair terms* contrasts with *villain's mind* as *words* may contrast with *thoughts* – like
A goodly apple rotten at the heart
(line 94).

If he will take it, so; if not, adieu,[65]
And for my love I pray you wrong me not.

ANTONIO

Yes, Shylock, I will seal unto this bond.   165

SHYLOCK

Then meet me forthwith at the notary's.
Give him direction for this merry bond,   Joke bond.
And I will go and purse the ducats straight,[66]
See to my house, left in the fearful[67] guard
Of an unthrifty knave; and presently   170
I 'll be with you.   [*Exit*

ANTONIO

           Hie thee,[68] gentle Jew.
[*To* BASSANIO] The Hebrew will turn Christian, he grows
     kind.

BASSANIO

I like not[69] fair terms and a villain's mind.

ANTONIO

Come on, in this there can be no dismay;
My ships come home a month before the day.   [*Exeunt* 175

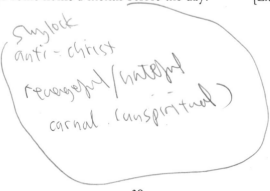

Shylock
anti - christ
revengeful / hateful
carnal. (unspiritual)

39

ACT TWO

(II.i) The Prince of Morocco, whose visit to Belmont was announced at the end of I.ii, now comes to ask Portia for her hand in marriage. He makes much of his appearance and his bravery, but Portia tells him he must, like the others, submit to the lottery of the caskets, and promise not to ask for the hand of any other woman if he loses. He agrees to these conditions.

1 *the Prince of MOROCCO* ... He is a native of North Africa, and his face is brown (*tawny*), not black. His attendants have skin of the same colour and are dressed as he is (*accordingly*). On the stage, the Prince of Morocco and his train enter on one side; Portia, her maid Nerissa, and her other attendants enter on the other.

2 *Mislike me not for* ... "Do not dislike me because of . . .".

3 *The shadowed* ... *sun* – "the dark ('shaded') mark of the brightly shining sun". The image here is of the sun as a lord who gives his servants a mark or badge to show that they belong to him; the sun is bright but the mark, a tawny skin, is dark.

4 *Phœbus'* – "the sun's".

5 *let us make incision* – literally "let us cut (our skins)". He is apparently

suggesting that he and his rival (he thinks there is only one) should cut themselves to find out *whose blood is reddest*, i.e. who is the braver and therefore the more worthy of Portia. Red blood was taken as a sign of courage.

6 *aspect* – "face, general appearance".

7 *feared* – "greatly frightened".

8 *our clime* – "our country" (literally "our climate").

9 *nice direction* – "very careful guidance".

10 *scanted* – "restricted".

11 *by his wit* – "in his wisdom".

12 *to yield* ... *wins me* – "to give myself as a wife to him who wins me".

13 *as fair* – "in as good a position", but also with a joke on *fair* as opposed to *dark*, since the Prince of Morocco has drawn attention to the darkness of his skin.

I pray you lead me to the caskets

ACT TWO

Scene I. Belmont. A room in Portia's house.

A flourish of cornets. Enter the Prince of MOROCCO,[1] *a tawny Moor, all in white, and three or four followers accordingly, with* PORTIA, NERISSA, *and their train.*

MOROCCO

Mislike me not for[2] my complexion,
The shadowed[3] livery of the burnished sun,
To whom I am a neighbour, and near bred.
Bring me the fairest creature northward born,
Where Phœbus'[4] fire scarce thaws the icicles,   5
And let us make incision[5] for your love,
To prove whose blood is reddest, his or mine.
I tell thee, lady, this aspect[6] of mine
Hath feared[7] the valiant; by my love I swear,
The best-regarded virgins of our clime[8]   10
Have loved it too. I would not change this hue,
Except to steal your thoughts, my gentle queen.

PORTIA

In terms of choice I am not solely led
By nice direction[9] of a maiden's eyes;
Besides, the lottery of my destiny   15
Bars me the right of voluntary choosing;
But if my father had not scanted[10] me,
And hedged me by his wit[11] to yield[12] myself
His wife, who wins me by that means I told you,
Your self, renownéd prince, then stood as fair[13]   20
As any comer I have looked on yet
For my affection.

MOROCCO

                Even for that I thank you;
Therefore I pray you lead me to the caskets

43

14 *the Sophy*, the Shah of Persia.

15 *That won . . . Solyman* – "who was victorious in three battles (*won three fields*) against Solyman (i.e. Suleiman the Magnificent), Sultan (of Turkey)". The Turks and the Persians were at war against one another in 1534.

16 *o'erstare . . . look* – "look for longer at the fiercest eyes that see, and look more fiercely than they look at me".

17 *alas the while!* – "how unhappy the time is!"

18 *Hercules and Lichas*. Hercules, a Greek hero of enormous strength, sent his companion Lichas to bring him a white garment which he intended to use during a sacrifice. The garment was poisoned, and from it he met his death. If these two *play at dice* to find who is *the better* (i.e. stronger, braver) *man*, luck might have it that the weaker man throws the better dice.

19 *Alcides*, another name for Hercules.

20 *be advised* – "think carefully".

21 *Nor will not* – "And I will not (speak to a woman afterwards in this way)."

22 *forward to the temple* – "let us go to the church", to take the oath he must swear to.

23 *blest or cursed'st* – "either the most blessed or the most cursed".

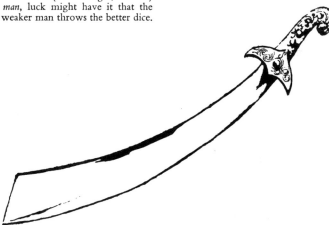

By this scimitar

To try my fortune. By this scimitar
That slew the Sophy,[14] and a Persian prince   25
That won[15] three fields of Sultan Solyman,
I would o'erstare[16] the sternest eyes that look,
Outbrave the heart most daring on the earth,
Pluck the young sucking cubs from the she-bear,
Yea, mock the lion when he roars for prey,   30
To win thee, lady. But alas the while ![17]
If Hercules and Lichas[18] play at dice,
Which is the better man, the greater throw
May turn by fortune from the weaker hand;
So is Alcides[19] beaten by his page,   35
And so may I, blind Fortune leading me,
Miss that which one unworthier may attain,
And die with grieving.

PORTIA

            You must take your chance,
And either not attempt to choose at all,
Or swear before you choose, if you choose wrong,   40
Never to speak to lady afterward
In way of marriage; therefore be advised.[20]

MOROCCO

Nor will not.[21] Come, bring me unto my chance.

PORTIA

First, forward to the temple;[22] after dinner
Your hazard shall be made.

MOROCCO

            Good fortune then,   45
To make me blest or cursed'st[23] among men !

                [*Sound of cornets. Exeunt*

(ii.ii) Shylock's manservant, Launcelot Gobbo, is trying to decide whether or not to leave his master's service; he discusses the matter with himself by making a conversation between his conscience and the devil. Old Gobbo, his father, almost blind, comes up to him but does not know him, and Launcelot teases him before he reveals himself. When Bassanio comes in, Launcelot, with his father's help, begs Bassanio to give him a place in his house; Bassanio agrees to do so, and sends him off.

Gratiano, a friend of Bassanio's, then comes in and begs to be allowed to accompany Bassanio to Belmont, Portia's house. Bassanio agrees, but on the condition that Gratiano behaves a little more soberly than he usually does.

1 *serve me to run* – "allow me to run away".

2 *the fiend*, i.e. the tempter, Satan. The imaginary conversation between the fiend and Gobbo's conscience is a joke on the old morality plays, in which virtues and vices were personified and acted like real people.

3 *scorn . . . with thy heels* – "spurn . . ., reject the idea completely".

4 *pack* – "go away".

5 *Fia!* – "Go ahead!"

6 *for the heavens* – "by heaven" (a strange oath for the devil to swear to).

7 *hanging about . . . heart:* the heart is the source of the affections, and conscience is spoken of as hanging on its neck, like a frightened wife. The phrase is meant to sound absurd.

8 *did something smack* – "had a rather bad flavour", i.e. was not perfect in every way.

9 *God bless the mark:* this phrase was used to excuse a remark which was in some way improper: "May God forgive me." In lines 21-2, *saving your reverence* has nearly the same meaning: "excuse this offensive remark".

10 *incarnation* for *incarnate* – "in the flesh"; Gobbo uses the word wrongly.

Sultan Solyman [15]

46

Scene II. Venice. (A street.

Enter LAUNCELOT GOBBO, *the clown, alone.*

parodying the 'morality play

LAUNCELOT

Certainly, my conscience will serve me to run[1] from this
Jew my master; the fiend[2] is at mine elbow, and tempts me,
saying to me, "Gobbo, Launcelot Gobbo, good Launcelot,"
or "good Gobbo", or "good Launcelot Gobbo, use your legs,
take the start, run away." My conscience says, "No; take   5
heed, honest Launcelot, take heed, honest Gobbo," or, as
aforesaid, "honest Launcelot Gobbo; do not run, scorn[3]
running with thy heels." Well, the most courageous fiend
bids me pack,[4] "Fia!"[5] says the fiend, "away!" says the fiend,
"for the heavens,[6] rouse up a brave mind," says the fiend, "and   10
run." Well, my conscience, hanging about[7] the neck of my
heart, says very wisely to me: "My honest friend Launcelot" –
being an honest man's son, or rather an honest woman's son,
for indeed my father did something smack,[8] something
grow to; he had a kind of taste – well, my conscience says   15
"Launcelot, budge not!" "Budge!" says the fiend. "Budge
not!" says my conscience. "Conscience," say I, "you counsel
well; fiend," say I, "you counsel well"; to be ruled by my
conscience, I should stay with the Jew my master, who (God
bless the mark)[9] is a kind of devil; and to run away from the   20
Jew I should be ruled by the fiend, who (saving your
reverence) is the devil himself; certainly the Jew is the very
devil incarnation,[10] and in my conscience, my conscience is
but a kind of hard conscience, to offer to counsel me to stay
with the Jew; the fiend gives the more friendly counsel: I   25
will run, fiend; my heels are at your commandment; I will run.

Enter old GOBBO *with a basket.*

GOBBO

Master young man, you I pray you, which is the way to
Master Jew's?

11 *my true-begotten father: true-begotten* is nonsense here since it is the son who is begotten by the father, not the other way round. This is more of Launcelot Gobbo's fooling.

12 *sand-blind* – "almost blind". Those who were completely blind were said to be *stone-blind*, and Launcelot invents a degree of blindness between the two: *gravel-blind*. (Gravel is small stones mixed together, as is often used for making paths.)

13 *try confusions* – "try to confuse". Launcelot is playing on the phrase *try conclusions*, which meant "carry out experiments".

14 *of no hand* – "in no direction at all"; this is more of Launcelot's nonsense, and completely confuses his father.

15 *sonties* – "saints".

16 *young* Master *Launcelot;* he gives himself a title which his father denies in the following lines. "Master" was used in addressing an educated man of the middle class.

17 *raise the waters* – (perhaps) "cause confusion", though the phrase may mean "bring the tears", i.e. "make him cry".

18 *No "master", sir*. The humour of the situation lies in Gobbo denying that his son is to be called "Master" and yet calling Gobbo "Master", etc., all the time.

19 *well to live* – "in good health".

20 *a* for *he,* a conversational form.

48

malapropism

LAUNCELOT [*Aside*]

O heavens! this is my true-begotten father,[11] who, being
more than sand-blind,[12] high gravel-blind, knows me not. I   30
will try confusions[13] with him.

GOBBO

Master young gentleman, I pray you, which is the way to
Master Jew's?

LAUNCELOT

Turn up on your right hand at the next turning, but at the
next turning of all on your left; marry, at the very next   35
turning turn of no hand,[14] but turn down indirectly to the
Jew's house.

GOBBO

By God's sonties,[15] 't will be a hard way to hit. Can you tell
me whether one Launcelot that dwells with him, dwell with
him or no?   40

LAUNCELOT

Talk you of young *Master* Launcelot?[16] [*Aside*] Mark me
now, now will I raise the waters.[17] [*To* GOBBO]. Talk you
of young *Master* Launcelot?

GOBBO

No "master", sir,[18] but a poor man's son. His father, though
I say 't, is an honest, exceeding poor man, and, God be   45
thanked, well to live.[19]

LAUNCELOT

Well, let his father be what a[20] will, we talk of young Master
Launcelot.

GOBBO

Your worship's friend and Launcelot, sir.

49

21 *ergo* – Latin for "therefore". Launcelot knows that it is a word used in argument, but possibly thinks that it is a verb, and means "reason it out".

22 *father* – "old man". A joke lies in the fact that Gobbo is in fact Launcelot's father.

23 *the Sisters Three*, the Fates, who were thought of in classical times as three women, one of whom spun the thread of life, another gave it to a man as his fate, and the third cut it off when his life was to end.

24 *staff . . . prop.* Gobbo uses these ideas as metaphors for "support", something on which he leans for help. His son pretends to misunderstand him, and asks whether he looks like a cudgel (see Glossary) or a post.

25 *hovel-post* – "centre-post for building a stack of corn".

26 *Alack the day!* A common expression of sorrow: "Alas (that I have lived to see) this day."

27 *father* can now be taken as either "old man" or "father".

28 *fail of the knowing me* – "not be able to recognize me".

29 *it is a wise . . . child.* Launcelot is apparently making fun of an old proverb: "It's a wise child that knows his own father".

LAUNCELOT

But I pray you, ergo[21] old man, ergo I beseech you, talk you   50
of young Master Launcelot?

GOBBO

Of Launcelot, an 't please your mastership.

LAUNCELOT

Ergo Master Launcelot. Talk not of Master Launcelot, father,[22]
for the young gentleman, according to fates and destinies, and
such odd sayings, the Sisters Three,[23] and such branches of   55
learning, is indeed deceased, or, as you would say in plain terms,
gone to heaven.

GOBBO

Marry, God forbid! The boy was the very staff[24] of my age,
my very prop.

LAUNCELOT [*Aside*]

Do I look like a cudgel or a hovel-post,[25] a staff, or a prop? –   60
Do you know me, father?

GOBBO

Alack the day![26] I know you not, young gentleman, but I pray
you tell me, is my boy, God rest his soul, alive or dead?

LAUNCELOT

Do you not know me, father?[27]

GOBBO

Alack, sir, I am sand-blind; I know you not.   65

LAUNCELOT

Nay, indeed, if you had your eyes you might fail of the knowing
me;[28] it is a wise[29] father that knows his own child. Well,
old man, I will tell you news of your son. [*Kneels with his back*

30 *truth will . . . long.* These are also proverbs.

31 *I am Launcelot . . . shall be.* It is not clear what Launcelot means by this; perhaps it is a meaningless play of words on a phrase from the Bible, "which was, and is, and is to come" (*Revelation*, iv.8), which he is reminded of on this religious occasion of blessing. Here *boy, son* and *child* mean almost the same thing, and the phrase therefore shows no change between the past and the future; this furthers the nonsense of the clowning.

32 *if thou be Launcelot.* Old Gobbo now begins to address Launcelot as *thou,* not *you,* since he is satisfied that Launcelot is his son; see Introduction, p. ix on this subject.

33 This action is traditional only; it is not written in the early editions of the play.

34 *worshipped might He be.* He adds this phrase after calling on God (*Lord!*) to make it sound more reverent. It may be compared with *saving your reverence* in lines 21–2 above, and line 115 below.

35 *fill-horse,* a horse used for pulling carts.

36 *grows backward* – "grows shorter", not longer.

37 *How dost . . . agree?* – "How do you and your master get along together?"

38 *'gree* for *agree.*

to GOBBO] Give me your blessing; truth will[30] come to light, murder cannot be hid long – a man's son may, but in the end 70 truth will out.

GOBBO [*placing his hands on* LAUNCELOT'S *head*]

Pray you, sir, stand up; I am sure you are not Launcelot my boy.

LAUNCELOT

Pray you, let 's have no more fooling about it, but give me your blessing; I am Launcelot[31] your boy that was, your son 75 that is, your child that shall be.

GOBBO

I cannot think you are my son.

LAUNCELOT

I know not what I shall think of that; but I am Launcelot, the Jew's man, and I am sure Margery your wife is my mother.

GOBBO

Her name is Margery indeed; I 'll be sworn, if thou be 80 Launcelot,[32] thou art mine own flesh and blood. [*He feels the back of* LAUNCELOT'S *head*][33] Lord! (worshipped might He be),[34] what a beard hast thou got! Thou hast got more hair on thy chin than Dobbin my fill-horse[35] has on his tail.

LAUNCELOT

It should seem, then, that Dobbin's tail grows backward.[36] 85 I am sure he had more hair of his tail than I have of my face, when I last saw him.

GOBBO

Lord, how art thou changed! How dost[37] thou and thy master agree? I have brought him a present; how 'gree[38] you now? 90

39 *set up my rest* – "made up my mind, determined". Launcelot then plays on the word *rest*, using it to mean "stop, remain".

40 *a very Jew* – "a Jew in every way".

41 This action is again traditional. Launcelot apparently confuses himself with his trick, and confuses fingers and ribs in what he says.

42 *me* – "on my behalf".

43 *rare* – "fine".

44 *You may* . . . Bassanio is just finishing giving orders to his man as he enters the stage.

45 *so hasted* – "done so quickly".

46 *put . . . to making* – "get . . . made up".

47 *Gramercy* – "Goodness!" To give the idea of confusion, father and son constantly interrupt one another in what follows.

48 *wouldst thou . . . me?* – "do you want anything of me?"

LAUNCELOT

Well, well; but for mine own part, as I have set up my rest[39]
to run away, so I will not rest till I have run some ground; my
master's a very Jew.[40] Give him a present? give him a halter!
I am famished in his service. [*He makes* GOBBO *feel the fingers
of his left hand, which he stretches out on his chest like ribs*][41] You   95
may tell every finger I have with my ribs. Father, I am glad
you are come; give me[42] your present to one Master Bassanio,
who indeed gives rare[43] new liveries; if I serve not him, I will
run as far as God has any ground. O rare fortune! here comes
the man; to him father, for I am a Jew if I serve the Jew any   100
longer.

> *Enter* BASSANIO *with* LEONARDO *and
> a follower or two*

BASSANIO

[*To one of the men*] You may[44] do so, but let it be so hasted[45]
that supper be ready at the farthest by five of the clock. See
these letters delivered, put[46] the liveries to making, and desire
Gratiano to come anon to my lodging.   [*Exit the man*   105

LAUNCELOT

To him, father.

GOBBO

[*To* BASSANIO] God bless your worship.

BASSANIO

Gramercy,[47] wouldst thou aught with me?[48]

GOBBO

Here's my son, sir, a poor boy –

LAUNCELOT

Not a poor boy, sir, but the rich Jew's man that would, sir –   110
as my father shall specify –

49 *infection.* Gobbo uses this wrongly for *affection* – "wish".

50 *the short . . . long is* – "briefly what I have to say is". (There is a similar modern English idiom: *the long and and the short of it is . . .*)

51 *are scarce cater-cousins* – "are not on friendly terms with each other". It is not clear what *cater* means; but *cousin* was used in Shakespeare's day for "friend", and here the meaning is clearly that they were no longer friends.

52 Launcelot perhaps means *old* to be *honest,* but by now he and his father have completely confused one another.

53 *frutify,* Launcelot's mistake for *certify* or a similar word.

54 *a dish of doves,* i.e. enough cooked doves to fill a dish. This is Gobbo's present to the man his son wants to work for, and having given it he can then make his request, his *suit.*

55 *impertinent,* Launcelot's mistake for *pertinent* – "concerning".

56 *What would you?* – "What do you want?"

57 *defect;* he means *effect* – "conclusion".

malapropism .

affection

GOBBO

He hath a great infection,[49] sir, (as one would say) to serve –

LAUNCELOT

Indeed, the short[50] and the long is, I serve the Jew, and have a desire – as my father shall specify –

GOBBO

His master and he (saving your worship's reverence) are 115 scarce cater-cousins,[51] –

LAUNCELOT

To be brief, the very truth is that the Jew, having done me wrong, doth cause me, – as my father (being, I hope, an old[52] man) shall frutify[53] unto you –

certify

GOBBO

I have here a dish of doves[54] that I would bestow upon your 120 worship, and my suit is –

LAUNCELOT

pertinent

In very brief, the suit is impertinent[55] to myself, as your worship shall know by this honest old man – and though I say it, though old man, yet, poor man, my father.

BASSANIO

One speak for both ! – What would you?[56]   125

LAUNCELOT

Serve you, sir.

GOBBO

That is the very defect[57] of the matter, sir.

58 *thou hast obtained thy suit* – "you have had your request granted".

59 *preferred* – "recommended".

60 *preferment* – "advancement"; he plays upon *prefer*.

61 *The old proverb;* this was "The grace of God is gear enough (i.e. sufficient provision)." Launcelot says this proverb is *parted*, i.e. divided, between Shylock and Bassanio: Shylock has enough (worldly property) but not, as he sees it, the grace of God.

62 *inquire My lodging out* – "find out where I am staying".

63 *guarded* – "ornamented"; but this is an uncertain honour since a brightly decorated coat suggests that he is going to be Bassanio's "fool", the servant who is there to make his master laugh. Bassanio praises him in line 136 for the wit he has shown in his use of a proverb: *Thou speak'st it well.*

64 *I have ne'er* ... Some points in this speech of Launcelot's are difficult to understand, but much can be explained if we realize that he continues to confuse his father by saying things which are the opposite of the truth. Thus, *I have ne'er a tongue in my head* suggests that he cannot be witty, and therefore get into Bassanio's service, because he has not even a tongue in his head, a statement which is, of course, not true.

65 *Well, if any man ... fortune.* Here again Launcelot aims to confuse: as he looks at his palm (a part of which is called the *table* in fortune-telling) he says that a man who has a luckier palm than he has will be fortunate indeed – but instead of saying *he* shall have good fortune, he says *I* shall ...; "Well, if there is any man in Italy who has a luckier palm than I have, and is prepared to swear with it on the Bible (i.e. is an honest man) – I (for *he*) shall indeed be fortunate."

66 *Go to* – "Well!"

67 *a simple line of life.* On the palm of the hand there is a line passing round the ball of the thumb; this was known as the line of life. Clear lines joining the ball of the thumb with the line of life were thought to indicate the number of wives a man would have. Launcelot calls his *simple*, meaning the opposite, i.e. that it is very complicated, and indicates many wives.

68 *aleven* for *eleven*, pronounced in a vulgar way.

69 *coming-in* – "income".

70 *scape* for *escape*.

71 *with the edge ... bed.* This may be another of Launcelot's surprises; we would expect to hear *edge of the sword*, or of something else equally hard, and instead we hear of something soft, *a feather-bed*.

72 *wench* – "girl".

73 *gear* – "business".

74 *in the twinkling:* this is short for *in the twinkling of an eye*, i.e. "in a moment; instantly".

75 *I pray thee;* Bassanio has been giving Leonardo instructions while Launcelot has been talking to his father.

76 *orderly bestowed* – "put away in an orderly fashion". Leonardo has to lay in stores for Bassanio's party.

58

BASSANIO

I know thee well; thou hast obtained thy suit,[58]
Shylock thy master spoke with me this day,
And hath preferred[59] thee, if it *be* preferment[60]   130
To leave a rich Jew's service, to become
The follower of so poor a gentleman.

LAUNCELOT

The old proverb[61] is very well parted between my master
Shylock and you, sir; you have "the grace of God", sir, and
he hath "enough".   135

BASSANIO

Thou speak'st it well; [*To* GOBBO] go, father, with thy son –
[*To* LAUNCELOT] Take leave of thy old master, and inquire
My lodging out.[62] [*To his followers*] Give him a livery
More guarded[63] than his fellows'; see it done.

LAUNCELOT

Father, in; – I cannot get a service, no! I have ne'er[64] a   140
tongue in my head. [*He looks at the palm of his hand*] Well, if
any man[65] in Italy have a fairer table which doth offer to swear
upon a book, I shall have good fortune! Go to,[66] here 's a
simple line of life,[67] here 's a small trifle of wives; alas!
fifteen wives is nothing, aleven[68] widows and nine maids is   145
a simple coming-in[69] for one man, and then to scape[70]
drowning thrice, and to be in peril of my life with the edge
of a feather-bed,[71] here are simple scapes. Well, if Fortune
be a woman, she 's a good wench[72] for this gear.[73] Father,
come; I 'll take my leave of the Jew in the twinkling.[74]   150

[*Exit with old* GOBBO

BASSANIO

I pray thee,[75] good Leonardo, think on this;
These things being bought and orderly bestowed,[76]

77 *I do feast . . . acquaintance* – "I am giving a feast tonight to the friends I value most highly (*best-esteemed*)".
78 *Hie thee* – "Hurry away".
79 *I have suit to you* – "I have a request to make of you".
80 *rude* – "rough in manner".
81 *they show . . . liberal* – "they appear rather too free".

82 *modesty* – "good manners". Bassanio fears that a journey to Belmont in Gratiano's company will not be successful unless Gratiano behaves a little more quietly than he usually does.

Return in haste, for I do feast[77] to-night
My best-esteemed acquaintance. Hie thee,[78] go!

LEONARDO

My best endeavours shall be done herein. 155

[*He begins to leave*

Enter GRATIANO

GRATIANO

Where 's your master?

LEONARDO

Yonder, sir, he walks. [*Exit*

GRATIANO

Signior Bassanio!

BASSANIO

Gratiano!

GRATIANO

I have suit to you.[79]

BASSANIO

You have obtained it.

GRATIANO

You must not deny me; I must go with you to Belmont. 160

BASSANIO

Why then you must – but hear thee, Gratiano;
Thou art too wild, too rude,[80] and bold of voice,
Parts that become thee happily enough,
And in such eyes as ours appear not faults.
But where thou art not known, why, there they show[81] 165
Something too liberal. Pray thee, take pain
To allay with some cold drops of modesty[82]
Thy skipping spirit, lest through thy wild behaviour

Belmont is much laddish

83 *misconstered* for *misconstrued* – "mis-
understood".

84 *habit* – "behaviour".

85 *while grace is saying* – "while grace
(a prayer before meals) is being
said".

86 *hood . . . hat.* In Shakespeare's day
people wore hats at meal-times, but
took them off, as Gratiano shows,
while grace was being said.

87 *the observance of civility* – "the
practices of good manners".

88 *sad ostent* – "serious appearance".

89 *grandam* – "grandmother".

(II.iii) Shylock's daughter, Jessica, says good-bye to Launcelot with real
regret, but takes the opportunity of giving him a letter to pass on to
Lorenzo, who is staying in Bassanio's house. She is in love with Lorenzo,
and regrets that she is a Jewess because this may make it difficult for her to
marry him.

I be misconstered[83] in the place I go to,
And lose my hopes.

GRATIANO

     Signior Bassanio, hear me: 170
If I do not put on a sober habit,[84]
Talk with respect, and swear but now and then,
Wear prayer-books in my pocket, look demurely,
Nay more, while grace is saying,[85] hood mine eyes[86]
Thus with my hat, and sigh and say "amen",   175
Use all the observance of civility[87]
Like one well studied in a sad ostent[88]
To please his grandam,[89] never trust me more.

BASSANIO

Well, we shall see your bearing.

GRATIANO

Nay, but I bar to-night; you shall not gauge me   180
By what we do to-night.

BASSANIO

     No, that were pity;
I would entreat you rather to put on
Your boldest suit of mirth, for we have friends
That purpose merriment. But fare you well;
I have some business.   185

GRATIANO

And I must to Lorenzo and the rest;
But we will visit you at supper-time.   [*Exeunt*

Scene III. Venice. A street.

Enter JESSICA *and* LAUNCELOT, *the clown.*

JESSICA

I am sorry thou wilt leave my father so;

63

1 *devil* links with *hell* in the same line.

2 *rob it . . . tediousness* – "took away from it something of its dullness".

3 *exhibit*. Gobbo's mistake for *inhibit* or *prohibit* – "prevent (me from using) my tongue".

4 *pagan*, i.e. not Christian.

5 *something* – "somewhat".

(II.iv) Gratiano and the rest are here seen planning a masque, i.e. a short play for which the actors wore masks and later mixed with the guests for dancing. When the actors came in, torch-bearers carried lighted torches before them, but in this instance these have not been arranged, and time is short. Launcelot brings in Jessica's letter, and Lorenzo learns that, disguised as a page, she plans to run away with him.

1 *in* – "during".

2 *All in an hour* – "very quickly", i.e. we shall be back within one hour.

SCENE IV]

Our house is hell, and thou, a merry devil,[1]
Didst rob it[2] of some taste of tediousness.
But fare thee well; [*She gives him some money*] there is a ducat
    for thee,
And Launcelot, soon at supper shalt thou see   5
Lorenzo, who is thy new master's guest;
Give him this letter, do it secretly;
And so farewell; I would not have my father
See me in talk with thee.

LAUNCELOT

Adieu! tears exhibit[3] my tongue, most beautiful pagan,[4]   10 *jew = inferior*
most sweet Jew! if a Christian do not play the knave and get
thee, I am much deceived; but adieu! these foolish drops do
something[5] drown my manly spirit; adieu!   [*Exit*

JESSICA

Farewell, good Launcelot.
Alack, what heinous sin is it in me   15
To be ashamed to be my father's child!
But though I am a daughter to his blood
I am not to his manners. O Lorenzo,
If thou keep promise I shall end this strife,
Become a Christian, and thy loving wife!   [*Exit*   20

Scene IV. Venice. A street.

Enter GRATIANO, LORENZO, SALERIO *and* SOLANIO.

LORENZO

Nay, we will slink away in[1] supper-time,
Disguise us at my lodging, and return
All in an hour.[2]

GRATIANO

We have not made good preparation.

65

3 *spoke us yet of* – either "yet ordered (for ourselves)"; or "spoken as yet about", in which case *us* is a misprint in the old editions for *as*.

4 *'Tis vile . . . ordered* – "It will be very bad unless it is arranged skilfully (*quaintly*)".

5 *undertook* for *undertaken*.

6 *An it . . . this* – "If it pleases you to break open (the seal of) this (letter)".

7 *the hand* – "the handwriting".

8 *writ* for *wrote*.

66

SALERIO

We have not spoke us yet of³ torch-bearers.   5

SOLANIO

'T is vile⁴ unless it may be quaintly ordered,
And better in my mind not undertook.⁵

LORENZO

'T is now but four of clock; we have two hours
To furnish us –

Enter LAUNCELOT, *with a letter.*
friend Launcelot, what 's the news?

LAUNCELOT

An it⁶ shall please you to break up this, it shall seem to signify.   10

LORENZO

I know the hand;⁷ in faith, 't is a fair hand,
And whiter than the paper it writ⁸ on
Is the fair hand that writ.

GRATIANO

Love-news, in faith.

LAUNCELOT

By your leave, sir.

LORENZO

Whither goest thou?   15

LAUNCELOT

Marry, sir, to bid my old master the Jew to sup to-night with
my new master the Christian.

9 *of* – "with".

10 *needs* – "of necessity".

11 *gentle* brings in a play of words on *Jew* in the previous line, since *gentle* and *Gentile* were not distinguished in pronunciation in Shakespeare's day. Jessica has already said that she plans to become a Christian (II.iii. 20).

12 *never dare . . . foot* – "let misfortune never dare to come her way".

13 *she*, i.e. misfortune.

14 *faithless* – "unbelieving", i.e. not Christian.

Gentile — Any non-Jews

LORENZO

Hold here, take this; [*He gives* LAUNCELOT *some money*] tell
gentle Jessica
I will not fail her; speak it privately,   [*Exit* LAUNCELOT
Go. – Gentlemen,   20
Will you prepare you for this masque to-night?
I am provided of⁹ a torch-bearer.

SALERIO

Ay, marry, I 'll be gone about it straight.

SOLANIO

And so will I.

LORENZO

Meet me and Gratiano   25
At Gratiano's lodging some hour hence.

SALERIO

'T is good we do so.   [*Exeunt* SALERIO *and* SOLANIO

GRATIANO

Was not that letter from fair Jessica?

LORENZO

I must needs¹⁰ tell thee all: she hath directed
How I shall take her from her father's house,   30
What gold and jewels she is furnished with,
What page's suit she hath in readiness.
If e'er the Jew her father come to heaven,
It will be for his gentle¹¹ daughter's sake;
And never dare¹² misfortune cross her foot,   35
Unless she¹³ do it under this excuse,
That she is issue to a faithless¹⁴ Jew;
Come, go with me, peruse this as thou goest.
Fair Jessica shall be my torch-bearer.   [*Exeunt*

(II.v) Launcelot gives Shylock Bassanio's invitation to supper, and Shylock accepts with some hesitation. He warns Jessica to guard the house well while he is away. Launcelot also lets Jessica know secretly that her lover, Lorenzo, may come for her that night.

1 *What, Jessica!* He calls this out to attract Jessica's attention.

2 *gormandize* – "eat a great deal"; but Launcelot said earlier (II.ii. 94) that he was *famished in* (Shylock's) *service*.

3 *rend apparel out* – "wear out clothes by treating them badly".

4 *Who bids thee call?* – "Who asked you to call out?" Launcelot pretends to be confused at Shylock speaking to him and calling out for Jessica at the same time.

5 *Your worship ... bidding* – "You, honoured sir, used to tell me that I was not allowed to do anything unless I was told to".

6 *bid forth* – "invited".

7 *wherefore* – "why".

8 *right loath* – "very unwilling".

Scene V. Venice. In front of Shylock's House.

Enter SHYLOCK *the Jew and* LAUNCELOT *his man, who was the clown.*

SHYLOCK

Well, thou shalt see, thy eyes shall be thy judge,
The difference of old Shylock and Bassanio; –
[*He calls out*] What, Jessica![1] – [*To* LAUNCELOT] thou shalt
  not gormandize[2]
As thou hast done with me – what, Jessica! –
And sleep, and snore, and rend apparel out.[3] –
Why, Jessica I say!

Lancelot is well treated.

LAUNCELOT

Why, Jessica!

SHYLOCK

Who bids thee call?[4] I do not bid thee call.

LAUNCELOT

Your worship[5] was wont to tell me I could do nothing without
bidding.

Enter JESSICA

JESSICA

Call you? what is your will?   10

SHYLOCK

Shylock

I am bid forth[6] to supper, Jessica;
There are my keys – but wherefore[7] should I go?
I am not bid for love; they flatter me;
But yet I'll go in hate, to feed upon
The prodigal Christian. Jessica, my girl,   *canabllistic*   15
Look to my house. – I am right loath[8] to go;

71

9 *some ill . . . rest* – "some trouble developing which will keep me from sleep".

10 *to–night* – "last night".

11 *reproach*, Launcelot's mistake for *approach*. Shylock takes him literally in the next line, saying he expected some *reproach*, "rebuke", from Bassanio, possibly because of the trouble Antonio is now in.

12 *it was not . . . afternoon* (line 26). Shylock said in lines 17-18 above that his dream about money-bags made him think that trouble was coming to him. Here Launcelot makes fun of such prophesying by pretending that certain signs have suggested to him that there was to be a masque that night. He knows for certain, in fact, because he must have overheard Lorenzo and Gratiano talking about it in the previous scene.

13 *fell a-bleeding* – "began to bleed".

14 *Black Monday*, a name for the first Monday after Easter.

15 *falling out* – "happening". From here to the end, the speech is deliberate nonsense.

16 *the wry-necked fife* – "the man with the twisted neck who plays the fife". The fife is played sideways, like the flute; hence the musician's twisted neck. The masquers sometimes walked in procession with musicians and torch-bearers along the street (*the public street*, line 31) to the place where the masque was to be presented.

17 *varnished faces* – "painted faces" or "masks", e.g. those of clowns. Shylock is probably implying that to wear these shows deception, since *varnished faces* cannot show the feelings behind them.

18 *casements* – "windows"; he speaks of them as the "ears" through which the house "listens".

19 *fopp'ry* – "foolery".

20 *By Jacob's staff*. In the Bible, Jacob says (*Genesis,* xxxii.10) that when he crossed the River Jordan he had nothing but his staff, and that now he has two companies of men. It is fitting that Shylock should swear by Jacob's staff, since his own experience will show how quickly worldly goods can come and go.

21 *I have . . . forth* – "I am not inclined to go out feasting".

22 *for all this* – "in spite of all that has been said (by Shylock, your father)".

23 *worth a Jewess' eye*. The expression "worth a Jew's eye", i.e. a great deal of money or profit, was proverbial. The earliest editions of the play indeed print *Jewes,* i.e. "Jew's", here, but *Jewess* is no doubt intended.

There is some ill[9] a-brewing towards my rest,
For I did dream of money-bags to-night.[10]

money concern

LAUNCELOT

I beseech you, sir, go; my young master doth expect your
reproach.[11]   20

SHYLOCK

So do I his.

LAUNCELOT

And they have conspired together; I will not say you shall
see a masque, but if you do, then it was not[12] for nothing
that my nose fell a-bleeding[13] on Black-Monday[14] last, at
six o'clock i' th' morning, falling out[15] that year on Ash-   25
Wednesday was four year in th' afternoon.

SHYLOCK

What, are there masques? – Hear you me, Jessica,
Lock up my doors, and when you hear the drum,
And the vile squealing of the wry-necked fife,[16]
Clamber not you up to the casements then,
Nor thrust your head into the public street
To gaze on Christian fools with varnished faces;[17]
But stop my house's ears – I mean my casements,[18]
Let not the sound of shallow fopp'ry[19] enter
My sober house. By Jacob's staff[20] I swear   35
I have[21] no mind of feasting forth to-night;
But I will go. [*To* LAUNCELOT] Go you before me, sirrah;
Say I will come.

no celebration/ Music uncivilised

LAUNCELOT

I will go before, sir.
[*To* JESSICA] Mistress, look out at window, for all this[22] –
There will come a Christian by   40
Will be worth a Jewess' eye.[23]   [*Exit*

73

24 *fool of Hagar's offspring*. Hagar was a servant of Abraham's wife, Sarah; she was an Egyptian, not a Jew, and her son Ishmael was an outcast (*Genesis* xvi).

25 *patch* – "foolish fellow".

26 *snail-slow in profit* – "very slow at improving himself".

27 *drones hive not with me* – "bees who do no work cannot make their hive with me". Much of the effect of Shylock's speeches lies in his use of imagery; cf. *my house's ears, snail-slow, the wild-cat,* above.

28 *His borrowed purse* – "the money he has borrowed". This is Bassanio, who is to borrow money through Antonio.

29 "*Fast bind, fast find*" – "If you make something safe, you will find it safe (when you want it again)".

30 *crost* (i.e. *crossed*) – "prevented".

(II.vi) Gratiano and Salerio, ready for the masque, are waiting for Lorenzo at an agreed place near Shylock's house. When Lorenzo comes, he calls out and Jessica appears above; she throws down some of her father's treasure for him to take away and then comes down to him, ready to run away from her father's house. They leave, but before Gratiano gets away, Antonio comes in and stops him; Antonio gives the news that the ship which is to take Bassanio to Belmont is ready to sail immediately.

1 *Lorenzo Desired . . . stand* – "Lorenzo asked us to wait". By a special arrangement, they are waiting for him in a shelter with a sloping roof (*penthouse*), ready to help him with his plans to get Jessica from her father. But Lorenzo is late for the meeting, and this surprises them, because *lovers ever run before the clock* (line 4), i.e. lovers are always early in their affairs.

SHYLOCK

What says that fool of Hagar's offspring?[24] ha?

JESSICA

His words were, "Farewell, mistress"; nothing else.

SHYLOCK

The patch[25] is kind enough, but a huge feeder,
Snail-slow in profit,[26] and he sleeps by day   45
More than the wild-cat; drones hive not with me,[27]
Therefore I part with him, and part with him
To one that I would have him help to waste
His borrowed purse.[28] Well, Jessica, go in –
Perhaps I will return immediately –   50
Do as I bid you; shut doors after you –
"Fast bind, fast find"[29] –
A proverb never stale in thrifty mind.   [Exit

JESSICA

Farewell; – and if my fortune be not crost,[30]
I have a father, you a daughter, lost.   [Exit   55

Scene VI. The same.

Enter GRATIANO *and* SALERIO, *dressed for the masque.*

GRATIANO

This is the penthouse under which Lorenzo
Desired[1] us to make stand.

SALERIO

His hour is almost past.

GRATIANO

And it is marvel he out-dwells his hour,
For lovers ever run before the clock.

2 *O ten times . . . unforfeited* (line 7) – "The doves (*pigeons*) that pull the chariot of Venus (goddess of love) fly ten times more quickly to confirm a newly-made contract of love than they would do to keep a long-standing promise (*faith unforfeited*), bound by firm agreement (*obligéd*)".

3 *That ever holds* – "That is always true". Gratiano goes on to give some examples to illustrate this general truth, that the beginning of an undertaking is more vigorous and enthusiastic than the end. The fact that his examples are not very interesting and add nothing to the plot serves to emphasise that the friends have nothing to do but wait.

4 *that* – "with which".

5 *untread . . . tedious measures* – "return with the same stately controlled paces".

6 *younger* – "fine young man".

7 *prodigal* – "person who is wasteful and careless". Shakespeare doubtless had in mind here the Bible story of the "prodigal son" (*Luke*, xv. 11–32), who wasted his father's money on expensive living, but was welcomed home by his father when he had lost everything.

8 *The scarféd bark* – "a ship decorated with flags"; it wears its flags like scarves.

9 *puts from* – "sets sail from, leaves".

10 *the strumpet wind*; the wind acts like a *strumpet* ("wicked woman") with the young prodigal, the ship.

11 *she*, i.e. the ship.

12 *over-weathered ribs* – "ribs (i.e. cross-pieces of wood round the bottom of the ship) worn out by rough weather".

13 *Lean* links with *ribs* in the previous line; the ribs of a person who is lean with hunger show beneath his skin.

14 *of this,* i.e. on this subject.

15 *your patience for,* i.e. "I ask you to be patient about", "please forgive me for".

16 *abode* – "delay".

17 *When you . . . you then* – "If at any time you want to play the part of thieves, and steal wives for yourselves, I'll wait (*watch*) as long for you."

18 *my father Jew.* Lorenzo hopes that Shylock will become his father-in-law, because he wants to marry Jessica.

19 *within* – "inside (the house)".

20 *above,* i.e. on the balcony at the back of the stage in a theatre of Shakespeare's day.

21 *Albeit* – "although".

SALERIO

O ten times[2] faster Venus' pigeons fly
To seal love's bonds new-made, than they are wont
To keep obligéd faith unforfeited!

GRATIANO

That ever holds;[3] who riseth from a feast
With that keen appetite that[4] he sits down?
Where is the horse that doth untread[5] again   10
His tedious measures with the unbated fire
That he did pace them first? All things that are,
Are with more spirit chaséd than enjoyed.
How like a younger[6] or a prodigal[7]
The scarféd bark[8] puts from[9] her native bay,   15
Hugged and embracéd by the strumpet wind![10]
How like the prodigal doth she[11] return
With over-weathered ribs[12] and ragged sails,
Lean,[13] rent, and beggared by the strumpet wind!

Enter LORENZO

SALERIO

Here comes Lorenzo; more of this[14] hereafter.   20

LORENZO

Sweet friends, your patience for[15] my long abode;[16]
Not I but my affairs have made you wait;
When you[17] shall please to play the thieves for wives,
I'll watch as long for you then. Approach –
Here dwells my father Jew.[18] Ho! who's within?[19]   25

Enter JESSICA *above,*[20] *in boy's clothes.*

JESSICA

Who are you? – tell me, for more certainty –
Albeit[21] I'll swear that I do know your tongue.

77

22 *the pains* – "your trouble (to do so)".

23 *exchange* – "change (into boy's clothes)".

24 *pretty follies* – "artful little tricks".

25 *Cupid*, the Roman god of love, usually represented as a boy with wings.

26 *torch-bearer*; the need for torch-bearers to go in front of the masquers has already been mentioned. (II.iv.5). And torches have often been associated with the rites of love; Cupid himself was sometimes shown carrying a torch which enflamed the hearts of men to love.

27 *hold a candle . . . shames* – "light up my shame (my disguise as a boy) for all to see".

28 *good sooth* – "indeed".

29 *light* – "immoral", with a word-play on *candle*, etc. in the previous lines.

30 *'t is an office of discovery* – "it (what you have suggested) is work that reveals"; Jessica does not want to reveal herself.

31 *garnish* – "garments".

32 *the close night . . . runaway* – "the night, which keeps secrets, is slipping away, playing the part of a runaway".

33 *we are stayed for* – "they are waiting for us".

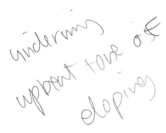

LORENZO

Lorenzo and thy love.

JESSICA

Lorenzo, certain, and my love indeed;
For who love I so much? and now who knows   30
But you Lorenzo whether I am yours?

LORENZO

Heaven and thy thoughts are witness that thou art.

JESSICA [*Throwing down a box*]

Here, catch this casket; it is worth the pains.[22]
I am glad 't is night – you do not look on me –
For I am much ashamed of my exchange;[23]   35
But love is blind, and lovers cannot see
The pretty follies[24] that themselves commit,
For if they could, Cupid[25] himself would blush
To see me thus transforméd to a boy.

LORENZO

Descend, for you must be my torch-bearer.[26]   40

JESSICA

What, must I hold a candle to my shames?[27]
They in themselves, good sooth,[28] are too too light.[29]
Why, 't is an office of discovery,[30] love,
And I should be obscured.

LORENZO

　　　　　　So are you, sweet,
Even in the lovely garnish[31] of a boy.   45
But come at once,
For the close night[32] doth play the runaway,
And we are stayed for[33] at Bassanio's feast.

34 *by my hood*; it is not clear why Gratiano swears by his hood. The phrase is an old one, and may come from the custom of using various kinds of hood to signify various professions; to swear by one's hood might have been to do so by one's professional honour. If so, Gratiano makes a joke of it in swearing by *his* hood, which is one worn by masquers.

35 *gentle* – "fine (woman)", with a joke on Gentile, as at II.iv.34; cf. note 11, p. 66 above.

36 *Beshrew me but I love . . .* – (literally) "May I be cursed if I do not love . . ."; but here *beshrew* is simply used for emphasis.

37 *Fie*, an exclamation of disgust. Antonio is apparently shocked at Gratiano being dressed up for the masque.

38 *is come about* – "has turned, veered". This means that the sailing-ship which was waiting for the wind can sail, and that Bassanio has to be found at once (*presently will go aboard* in the next line).

39 *on 't* – "of it".

stealing (handwritten annotation)

JESSICA

I will make fast the doors, and gild myself
With some more ducats, and be with you straight.   50

[*Exit above*

GRATIANO

Now, by my hood,[34] a gentle,[35] and no Jew.

LORENZO

Beshrew me but I love[36] her heartily;
For she is wise, if I can judge of her;
And fair she is, if that mine eyes be true;
And true she is, as she hath proved herself:
And therefore like herself, wise, fair, and true,
Shall she be placéd in my constant soul.   55

love without moralry. but framed in moralty ideas (handwritten annotation)

Enter JESSICA, *below.*

[*To* JESSICA] What, art thou come? – On, gentlemen, away!
Our masquing mates by this time for us stay.
Exit with JESSICA *and* SALERIO; GRATIANO *is about to follow*
them.

Enter ANTONIO

ANTONIO

Who 's there?   60

GRATIANO

Signior Antonio?

ANTONIO

Fie,[37] fie, Gratiano! where are all the rest?
'T is nine o'clock; our friends all stay for you.
No masque to-night – the wind is come about;[38]
Bassanio presently will go aboard;
I have sent twenty out to seek for you.   65

change in direction (handwritten annotation)

GRATIANO

I am glad on 't;[39] I desire no more delight
Than to be under sail, and gone to-night.

[*Exeunt*

(II.vii) This is the first of three scenes in which suitors for Portia's hand make a choice from among the caskets, in accordance with the wishes of her father at the time of his death (I.ii.24 ff.). After considerable thought, the Prince of Morocco chooses the golden casket, and finds inside a skull and a scroll of paper. On the paper are verses warning the reader against being misled by outward appearances. The prince has lost his chance in the lottery, and sadly leaves Belmont; Portia is not sorry.

1 *their trains* – "lines of attendants following them".

2 *discover* – "reveal".

3 *who* – "which"; *who* sounds well with *gold*; cf. *which* with *silver* in line 6 below.

4 *dull . . . blunt*; dull is the opposite of "*bright* in colour", and can also mean "blunt of edge"; blunt meant "frank in speech" and also "base". There are therefore two plays on words here.

5 *withal* – "as well".

6 *fair advantages* – "good profits".

7 *to shows of dross* – "for displays of what is worthless" (for *dross* see Glossary). Much of the imagery in this scene is, as we would expect, associated with the metals of the caskets; *gold* is linked with *riches* and *royalty* (the Prince of Morocco speaks of his mind as *golden* in this line); *silver* suggests *cold purity* (the silver light of the moon and the virgin purity of Diana the moon goddess) and *equity* (– "Who chooseth me shall get as much as he deserves" is the inscription on the silver casket); *lead* is heavy and unattractive to outward appearances, but has a value of its own. Morocco thinks over the possible meanings of these suggestions in the lines which follow.

8 *nor . . . nor* – "neither . . . nor".

Scene VII. Belmont. A room in Portia's house.

Flourish of cornets. Enter PORTIA *with* MOROCCO *and both their trains.*[1]

PORTIA [*To her attendants*]

Go, draw aside the curtains and discover[2]
The several caskets to this noble prince: –
[*To* MOROCCO] Now make your choice.

MOROCCO

This first of gold, who[3] this inscription bears:
"Who chooseth me shall gain what many men desire."   5
The second silver, which this promise carries:
"Who chooseth me shall get as much as he deserves."
This third, dull[4] lead, with warning all as blunt,
"Who chooseth me must give and hazard all he hath."
How shall I know if I do choose the right?   10

PORTIA

The one of them contains my picture, prince;
If you choose that, then I am yours withal.[5]

MOROCCO

Some god direct my judgement! let me see,
I will survey th' inscriptions back again; –
What says this leaden casket?   15
"Who chooseth me must give and hazard all he hath."
Must give – for what? for lead, hazard for lead!
This casket threatens – men that hazard all
Do it in hope of fair advantages;[6]
A golden mind stoops not to shows of dross,[7]   20
I 'll then nor[8] give nor hazard aught for lead.
What says the silver with her virgin hue?

83

9 *even* – "fair".

10 *rated by thy estimation* – "judged according to your own valuation of yourself".

11 *a weak disabling* – "poor discrediting". To believe that his own worth, even as he values it himself, would not be enough to win the lady seems to bring discredit on his person.

12 *graved* for *engraved*.

13 *this shrine ... saint.* Morocco is so filled with passionate love that he begins to use the language of religion in talking of Portia: "this image (*shrine*, as if she were a saint), this mortal, living (*breathing*) saint".

14 *Hyrcanian deserts*, a desert region south of the Caspian Sea, famous for its wildness.

15 *vasty wilds* – "vast wild regions". These desert places are, he says, now like main roads (*thoroughfares*), being constantly used by Portia's suitors. Morocco is particularly given to such overstatements as this. He now turns from deserts to seas.

16 *The watery kingdom*, i.e. the sea.

17 *spets* for *spits*; this is how Morocco describes a storm at sea, with the rising head (of the waves) spitting in the face of heaven.

18 *Is 't like* – "Is it likely".

19 *'t were* – "it would be".

20 *so base a thought*; this is a piece of word-play, since lead is a *base* metal.

21 *it were* – "it (*lead*) would be".

22 *To rib ... grave* – "to enclose her winding-cloth in the dark grave". It was the custom in Shakespeare's day to wrap dead bodies in waxed cloth (*cerecloth*) and then encase them in lead.

23 *a gem*; Morocco speaks of Portia as a precious stone fit only for a setting in gold; her picture should therefore be in the gold box.

24 *A coin.* This coin was in fact called an angel; on one side it had a figure of the archangel Michael treading on a dragon.

25 *that 's insculped upon* – "that (the figure) is engraved on it (the golden coin)". By contrast he hopes that the angel Portia, or in fact her picture, lies inside the gold box (*a golden bed*).

A coin that bears the figure of an angel
Stamped in gold [24]

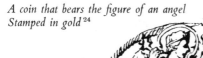

"Who chooseth me shall get as much as he deserves."
As much as he deserves! – Pause there, Morocco,
And weigh thy value with an even[9] hand; –   25
If thou be'st rated by thy estimation,[10]
Thou dost deserve enough, and yet enough   *consider one's*
May not extend so far as to the lady;   *self very*
And yet to be afeard of my deserving   *worth)*.
Were but a weak disabling[11] of myself.   30
As much as I deserve! – why, that 's the lady!
I do in birth deserve her, and in fortunes,
In graces, and in qualities of breeding;
But more than these, in love I do deserve –
What if I strayed no further, but chose here?   35
Let 's see once more this saying graved[12] in gold:
"Who chooseth me shall gain what many men desire";
Why, that 's the lady – all the world desires her.
From the four corners of the earth they come
To kiss this shrine,[13] this mortal breathing saint.   40
The Hyrcanian deserts,[14] and the vasty wilds[15]
Of wide Arabia are as throughfares now
For princes to come view fair Portia.
The watery kingdom,[16] whose ambitious head
Spets[17] in the face of heaven, is no bar   45
To stop the foreign spirits, but they come
As o'er a brook to see fair Portia.
One of these three contains her heavenly picture.
Is 't like[18] that lead contains her? – 't were[19] damnation
To think so base a thought;[20] it were[21] too gross   50
To rib[22] her cerecloth in the obscure grave; –
Or shall I think in silver she 's immured,
Being ten times undervalued to tried gold?
O sinful thought! never so rich a gem[23]
Was set in worse than gold. They have in England   55
A coin[24] that bears the figure of an angel
Stamped in gold, but that 's insculped upon;[25]
But here an angel in a golden bed

26 *thrive I . . . may* – "let me prosper as I may".

27 *form* – "picture".

28 *A carrion Death* – "A skull", which reminds him of death; he has been too bold in his reasoning, and risked too much.

29 *glisters* – "glitters". This line is a well-known proverb.

30 *But my . . . behold* – "only to look on my outside". This is evidently the outside of the casket or of anything made of gold; outward show is less important than what is inside, and men have given their lives for the show of riches.

31 *Your answer . . . inscrolled* – "an answer like this for you would not have been written on this scroll".

32 *your suit is cold* – "your offer of marriage is without effect".

33 *farewell, heat . . . frost.* There is said to have been a common expression, "Farewell, frost", said on the parting of anything which was disagreeable or unwelcome. Morocco inverts this saying, and refers to the *heat* of his passion for the beautiful Portia.

34 *a tedious leave* – "a long drawn-out farewell".

35 *part* – "leave, depart".

36 *complexion* – "character".

(II.viii) Salerio and Solanio here exchange the latest news. Shylock is in a rage over the flight of his daughter and the loss of the property she took with her. A ship has been lost off the English coast, and some fear that it is one of Antonio's. When Bassanio and Antonio said good-bye to one another, Antonio was deeply moved and begged Bassanio not to worry about the bond with Shylock.

1 *under sail* – "moving" (of a ship).

Lies all within. – Deliver me the key;
Here do I choose, and thrive I[26] as I may!   60

PORTIA

There, take it, prince, and if my form[27] lie there,
Then I am yours!   [*He unlocks the golden casket*

MOROCCO

O hell! what have we here?
A carrion Death,[28] within whose empty eye
There is a written scroll; – I'll read the writing.

All that glisters[29] is not gold;
Often have you heard that told.
Many a man his life hath sold
But my[30] outside to behold –
Gilded tombs do worms infold;
Had you been as wise as bold,
Young in limbs, in judgement old,
Your answer[31] had not been inscrolled –
Fare you well; your suit is cold.[32]

Cold indeed and labour lost;
Then, farewell, heat,[33] and welcome, frost!   75
Portia, adieu! I have too grieved a heart
To take a tedious leave;[34] thus losers part.[35]

[*Exit with his train*

PORTIA

A gentle riddance. [*To her attendants*] Draw the curtains; go; –
Let all of his complexion[36] choose me so.   [*Exeunt*

Scene VIII. Venice. A street.

Enter SALERIO *and* SOLANIO

SALERIO

Why, man, I saw Bassanio under sail;[1]
With him is Gratiano gone along,
And in their ship I am sure Lorenzo is not.

2 *The villain ... duke.* Shylock, returning to his house, found his
daughter fled with Lorenzo, and
much of his money gone too.
Solanio tells how Shylock appealed
to the Duke of Venice about this
(*with outcries raised the Duke*), and
how Bassanio's ship was searched
in vain.

3 *certified* – "assured".

4 *a passion* – "an outburst of passionate words". Shylock's *passion* shocks
Solanio because it speaks in one
breath of Shylock's daughter and
his money.

5 *double ducats*, coins worth twice the
amount of a ducat.

6 *Let good ... day* – "Good Antonio
must see to it that he keeps (the
promise of the bond on) the agreed
day". He must not *break his day*
(I.iii.157).

7 *well remembered* – "I am glad you
remembered that". The point about
Antonio's bond has reminded
Salerio of something.

8 *reasoned* – "talked".

9 *part* – "separate"; these *narrow
seas* are the Straits of Dover and the
seas near by.

in a gondola

88

Shylock's
loss of flesh & blood
'pound of flesh'
and hence t...

SOLANIO

The villain[2] Jew with outcries raised the Duke,
Who went with him to search Bassanio's ship.   5

SALERIO

He came too late; the ship was under sail;
But there the Duke was given to understand
That in a gondola were seen together
Lorenzo and his amorous Jessica.
Besides, Antonio certified[3] the Duke   10
They were not with Bassanio in his ship.

SOLANIO

I never heard a passion[4] so confused,
So strange, outrageous, and so variable,
As the dog Jew did utter in the streets:
"My daughter! O my ducats! O my daughter!   15
Fled with a Christian! O my Christian ducats!
Justice, the law, my ducats, and my daughter!
A sealéd bag, two sealéd bags of ducats,
Of double ducats,[5] stolen from me by my daughter!
And jewels, two stones, two rich and precious stones,   20
Stolen by my daughter! Justice! find the girl!
She hath the stones upon her, and the ducats!"

SALERIO

Why all the boys in Venice follow him,
Crying, his stones, his daughter, and his ducats.

SOLANIO

Let good[6] Antonio look he keep his day   23
Or he shall pay for this.

SALERIO

                    Marry, well remembered,[7] –
I reasoned[8] with a Frenchman yesterday,
Who told me, in the narrow seas that part[9]

89

10 *there miscarried . . . fraught* – "a ship from our country, laden with rich cargo (*richly fraught*), was wrecked (*miscarried*)".

11 *Slubber not business* – "do not carry out your business carelessly and hurriedly".

12 *stay . . . time* – "wait until time has brought your business to a successful conclusion (*riping*)".

13 *for* – "as for".

14 *mind of love* – "loving mind, mind full of the thoughts of love".

15 *fair ostents* – "fine displays".

16 *there* – "then, at that point (in what he was saying)".

17 *with affection . . . sensible* – "with remarkably apparent affection". This brief episode has not enough material for a separate scene, but, as reported by Salerio, it is most moving and effective. Antonio is clearly moved to sorrow at parting with his close friend Bassanio, yet, because of their friendship, he does not want Bassanio to do anything to please him which will spoil Bassanio's chances in the courtship of Portia.

18 *quicken . . . heaviness* – "lighten the sadness which he holds so closely to himself ('embraces')".

19 *Do we so* – "Let us do so".

Reminder by ironing samples it yet it not enter in your mind

The French and English, there miscarried[10]
A vessel of our country, richly fraught;   30
I thought upon Antonio when he told me,
And wished in silence that it were not his.

SOLANIO

You were best to tell Antonio what you hear;
Yet do not suddenly, for it may grieve him.

SALERIO

A kinder gentleman treads not the earth;   *praise of Antonio*
I saw Bassanio and Antonio part;   35
Bassanio told him he would make some speed
Of his return. He answered, "Do not so;
Slubber not business[11] for my sake, Bassanio,
But stay[12] the very riping of the time,   40
And for[13] the Jew's bond which he hath of me,
Let it not enter in your mind of love.[14]
Be merry, and employ your chiefest thoughts
To courtship, and such fair ostents[15] of love
As shall conveniently become you there."   45
And even there,[16] his eye being big with tears,
Turning his face, he put his hand behind him,
And with affection[17] wondrous sensible
He wrung Bassanio's hand, and so they parted.

laid back nature in comparison with Shylock

SOLANIO

I think he only loves the world for him.   50
I pray thee let us go and find him out
And quicken[18] his embracéd heaviness
With some delight or other.

SALERIO

Do we so.[19]   [*Exeunt*

(II.ix) Portia's second suitor, the Prince of Arragon, now comes to try his luck. He studies the writing on each of the caskets, and, after some reasoning, chooses the one made of silver. In it he finds a disgusting portrait, and he is shown that he was too much attracted by outward appearances to be successful. As soon as he leaves, a message is brought by a young man who tells that his lord, yet another suitor, will soon be there. Portia hopes that this will be Bassanio.

1 *Servitor* – "servant".

2 *straight* – "at once".

3 *The Prince ... oath.* This prince is another suitor for Portia's hand in marriage. First, as with the Prince of Morocco (II.i.44), he has to make a solemn oath at the temple.

4 *election* – "choice".

5 *that wherein I am contained* – "the one which contains me (i.e. my picture)".

6 *unfold to* – "reveal to, tell".

7 *so have I addressed me* – "I have prepared myself in this way", i.e. by promising to keep the conditions before coming to make his choice.

8 *fortune* – "good luck".

Scene IX. Belmont. A room in Portia's house.

Enter NERISSA *and a Servitor.*[1]

NERISSA

Quick, quick, I pray thee, draw the curtain straight;[2]
The Prince[3] of Arragon hath ta'en his oath,
And comes to his election[4] presently.

A flourish of cornets. Enter the Prince of ARRAGON, *his
train, and* PORTIA.

PORTIA

Behold, there stand the caskets, noble prince;
If you choose that wherein I am contained[5]   5
Straight shall our nuptial rites be solemnized.
But if you fail, without more speech, my lord,
You must be gone from hence immediately.

ARRAGON

I am enjoined by oath to observe three things: –
First, never to unfold to[6] anyone   10
Which casket 't was I chose; next, if I fail
Of the right casket, never in my life
To woo a maid in way of marriage;
Lastly,
If I do fail in fortune of my choice,   15
Immediately to leave you, and be gone.

PORTIA

To these injunctions every one doth swear
That comes to hazard for my worthless self.

ARRAGON

And so have I addressed me[7] – fortune[8] now
To my heart's hope! – Gold, silver, and base lead.   20

9 *You shall look fairer* – "You will have to look more beautiful"; he is addressing the leaden casket.

10 *that "many" . . . show* – "that word 'many' may be meant for (*By*) the foolish (*fool*) multitude, i.e. ordinary people, who choose only by outward appearances (*by show*)".

11 *fond* – "foolish".

12 *the martlet*, i.e. the house-martin, a bird which builds a nest of mud and straw high up under the roof on the outside walls of houses. It seems to have, therefore, little protection in bad weather (it *Builds in the weather*, line 29).

13 *Even in . . . casualty* – "in the very power (*force*) and path of mischance", i.e. the martin builds, it seems, just where there is least protection.

14 *jump* – "agree".

15 *rank me* – "take up my position".

16 *the stamp of merit*. The image here is of a *stamp* or official mark on some written agreement, proving that it is genuine. Arragon says he will not try to cheat Fortune by pretending to have great honour without meriting a proper claim to it. To do so would be to *wear an undeservéd dignity* (line 40).

17 *estates* – "position of high rank".

18 *degrees* – "social position".

19 *clear* – "pure", i.e. uncorrupted.

20 *purchased* – "acquired".

21 *the wearer*, i.e. the person enjoying the honour.

22 *How many . . . bare!* – "How many people would keep their hats on who now stand bareheaded". People took their hats off in the presence of their masters or superiors, and if honour went to those who merited it, many who are now servants would be masters.

23 *How much . . . honour!* – "How many who deserve to be nothing but poor peasants (*low peasantry*) would then be picked out (*gleaned*) from those who are truly the children of noble parents (*the true seed of honour*)". The image of gleaning corn is continued in *seed*, and *chaff* in the following line.

24 *ruin of the times* – "those which (hard) times have ruined".

25 *be new-varnished* – "appear bright again", once more showing their nobility. As many who are now honoured do not deserve to be, so many who are not honoured would be so if outward appearance always agreed with what lies beneath.

26 *I will assume desert* – "I will take what I deserve". But what he finds in the casket, a horrible portrait of a sub-normal person, is, he says (line 57), *much unlike my hopes and my deservings*.

"Who chooseth me must give and hazard all he hath." –
You shall look fairer,[9] ere I give or hazard.
What says the golden chest? ha! let me see,
"Who chooseth me shall gain what many men desire." –
What many men desire – that "many"[10] may be meant
By the fool multitude that choose by show,
Not learning more than the fond[11] eye doth teach,
Which pries not to th' interior, but, like the martlet,[12]
Builds in the weather on the outward wall,
Even in[13] the force and road of casualty.   30
I will not choose what many men desire,
Because I will not jump[14] with common spirits,
And rank me[15] with the barbarous multitudes.
Why, then, to thee, thou silver treasure house,
Tell me once more what title thou dost bear: 35
"Who chooseth me shall get as much as he deserves."
And well said, too; for who shall go about
To cozen Fortune, and be honourable
Without the stamp of merit?[16] Let none presume
To wear an undeservéd dignity;   40
O that estates,[17] degrees,[18] and offices,
Were not derived corruptly, and that clear[19] honour
Were purchased[20] by the merit of the wearer![21]
How many[22] then should cover that stand bare!
How many be commanded that command!   45
How much[23] low peasantry would then be gleaned
From the true seed of honour! and how much honour
Picked from the chaff and ruin of the times,[24]
To be new-varnished![25] – Well, but to my choice.
"Who chooseth me shall get as much as he deserves" –   50
I will assume desert;[26] give me a key for this,
And instantly unlock my fortunes here.

[*He opens the silver casket*

PORTIA

Too long a pause for that which you find there.

27 *schedule* – "scroll".

28 *distinct offices* – "duties of different kinds". Later in the play, Portia slips easily into the part of a lawyer, as this proverbial remark of hers suggests she might.

29 *this*, i.e. the silver of the casket. A phrase in the Bible (*Psalm* xii.6) speaks of silver as being refined seven times in the furnace.

30 *shadows*. This word clearly continues the idea of *appearances*, which is the theme of the silver casket; a shadow is only an appearance, not a reality. But it is not clear whether *shadow* here means "picture" or simply anything which is without substance.

31 *I wis* – "indeed"; the phrase is written as if it literally meant "I know".

32 *Silvered o'er*: this phrase also continues the idea of appearance as opposed to reality, and again it is not very clear. It probably means (1) white-haired, and therefore apparently wise and experienced but in fact not so; and (2) covered in silver, like this disgusting portrait enclosed in a silver casket.

33 *I will . . . head* – "you will always have a fool's head like mine (whoever you happen to marry)".

34 *sped* – "disposed of".

35 *Still more . . .* Before he leaves, Arragon makes a little speech in the same verse rhythm as that of the verses on the scroll. Although his situation is, for him at least, somewhat tragic, this trick of the verse-form may possibly suggest that it is not to be taken too seriously. Morocco also copies the form of the verses he reads, but for only two lines (II.vii.74–5).

36 *By the time . . . here* – "for as long as I stay here".

37 *Sweet* for "Sweet lady".

38 *wroth*. This must stand for *ruth* or *rue* – "grief".

39 *Thus hath . . . moth*. This was a proverbial expression; the light-minded person (*the moth*) has been attracted by the brightly shining object (the flame of *the candle*), and has come to grief (singed his wings).

ARRAGON

What 's here? the portrait of a blinking idiot
Presenting me a schedule![27] I will read it.
How much unlike art thou to Portia!   55
How much unlike my hopes and my deservings!
"Who chooseth me shall have as much as he deserves"!
Did I deserve no more than a fool's head?
Is that my prize? are my deserts no better?   60

PORTIA

To offend and judge are distinct offices,[28]
And of opposéd natures.

ARRAGON

What is here?
[He reads from the scroll] The fire seven times
        tried this;[29]
            Seven times tried that judgement is
            That did never choose amiss.   65
            Some there be that shadows[30] kiss;
            Such have but a shadow's bliss.
            There be fools alive, I wis,[31]
            Silvered o'er,[32] and so was this.
            Take what wife you will to bed,   70
            I will[33] ever be your head.
            So be gone; you are sped.[34]

            Still more[35] fool I shall appear
            By the time[36] I linger here;
            With one fool's head I came to woo,   75
            But I go away with two.
            Sweet,[37] adieu! I 'll keep my oath,
            Patiently to bear my wroth.[38]

                        [Exit ARRAGON with his train

PORTIA

Thus hath[39] the candle singed the moth;

40 *deliberate fools*, i.e. fools who "deliberate", use reason instead of following the deepest feelings of their hearts.

41 *They have . . . lose* – "they have only enough wisdom to lose by using their reason (*wit*)".

42 *heresy* – "lie".

43 *Hanging . . . destiny* – "Fate decides what happens to one in hanging or marrying"; (*goes* is for *go*). This is a proverb; the meaning emphasized here is that what decides is Fate, not Reason (*wit*) such as Arragon's.

44 *What would my lord?* – "what does 'my lord' want?" Portia calls the servant "*my lord*" as a joking reply to his calling her "*my lady*".

45 *before* – "in front".

46 *sensible regreets* – "greetings which are real", not just fine words spoken without feeling.

47 *commends* – "compliments".

48 *breath* – "speech".

49 *likely* – "promising, hopeful".

50 *costly* – "splendid". April days in England are often a mixture of sunshine and rain which promise the coming of summer.

51 *fore-spurrer*: one who spurs (i.e. hastens on horseback) in front of another.

52 *afeard* – "afraid".

53 *kin to thee* – "relative of yours", which would explain why the servant praised the newcomer so highly.

54 *high-day wit* – "fine words", not everyday speech but something special.

55 *post* – "messenger".

56 *mannerly* – "in such a grand manner".

57 *Bassanio . . . be!* The earliest editions of the play have this line punctuated in a number of different ways. If the one given here is correct, the line must mean: "Let it be (or: This is indeed) Bassanio, if you, Lord Love (i.e. Cupid, mentioned by Portia in the line before), wish it to be so!"

O these deliberate fools![40] when they do choose,   80
They have[41] the wisdom by their wit to lose.

NERISSA

The ancient saying is no heresy,[42]
Hanging and wiving goes by destiny.[43]

PORTIA

Come, draw the curtain, Nerissa.

Enter Messenger.

MESSENGER

Where is my lady?

PORTIA

Here; what would my lord?[44]   85

MESSENGER

Madam, there is alighted at your gate
A young Venetian, one that comes before[45]
To signify th' approaching of his lord,
From whom he bringeth sensible regreets,[46]
To wit, besides commends[47] and courteous breath,[48]   90
Gifts of rich value. Yet I have not seen
So likely[49] an ambassador of love.
A day in April never came so sweet   *precurza of summer*
To show how costly[50] summer was at hand,
As this fore-spurrer[51] comes before his lord.   95

PORTIA

No more, I pray thee; I am half afeard[52]
Thou wilt say anon he is some kin to thee,[53]
Thou spend'st such high-day wit[54] in praising him.
Come, come Nerissa, for I long to see
Quick Cupid's post[55] that comes so mannerly.[56]   100

NERISSA

Bassanio,[57] Lord Love, if thy will it be!   [*Exeunt*

99

ACT THREE

(III.i) Salerio and Solanio (whose part in the plot is often to recount events taking place outside Venice) tell of the wreck of another of Antonio's ships. Shylock comes up to them lamenting the loss of his daughter; and, when Antonio's bad luck is mentioned, Shylock makes it clear that he will take the forfeit if Antonio fails to redeem his bond. In a passionate speech, Shylock shows how a Jew's humanity is the same as a Christian's. One of Antonio's servants calls Salerio and Solanio away and Shylock's friend Tubal enters, bringing news that Antonio has lost yet another ship and is likely to be ruined. This gives Shylock some pleasure, and he prepares to take immediate action against Antonio.

1 *yet it ... unchecked* – "it (the rumour) continues to be put about there without being denied (*unchecked*)".

2 *of rich lading* – "with a rich cargo".

3 *the narrow seas*, i.e. the English Channel.

4 *flat*, i.e. shallow part of the sea.

5 *my gossip Report*. Rumour (*Report*) is personified as a *gossip*, an old woman who passes on rumours.

6 *that*, i.e. the news of the wreck of one of Antonio's ships.

7 *knapped ginger* – "nibbled (roots of) ginger". It seems that old women in England were once particularly fond of ginger, possibly because it was felt to be warming to the stomach.

8 *slips of prolixity* – "slipping into a very complicated style of speaking", leaving the *plain highway of talk*, "the open road of plain speaking", mentioned in what follows.

9 *Come ... stop* "Well, where is the full stop?"; despite Solanio's assurance that he will speak simply, he has begun so complicated a sentence that Salerio fears it will never end, reach a full stop.

10 *"amen"* – "so let it be", the usual ending to Christian prayers. Sometimes people made the sign of the cross as they said "Amen", and Solanio plays on this idea when he uses the word *cross*, meaning "go across, prevent from attaining success", in the next clause. By saying "amen" he has made Salerio's wish his own prayer.

11 *betimes* – "in good time".

ACT THREE

Scene I. Venice. A street.

Enter SOLANIO *and* SALERIO.

SOLANIO

Now what news on the Rialto?

SALERIO

Why, yet it[1] lives there unchecked, that Antonio hath a ship
of rich lading[2] wrecked on the narrow seas[3] – the Goodwins,
I think they call the place, a very dangerous flat,[4] and fatal,
where the carcases of many a tall ship lie buried, as they   5
say – if my gossip Report[5] be an honest woman of her word.

SOLANIO

I would she were as lying a gossip in that[6] as ever knapped
ginger,[7] or made her neighbours believe she wept for the
death of a third husband. But it is true, without any slips
of prolixity,[8] or crossing the plain highway of talk, that the   10
good Antonio, the honest Antonio – O that I had a title
good enough to keep his name company! –

SALERIO

Come, the full stop.[9]

SOLANIO

Ha! what sayest thou? – why the end is, he hath lost a ship.

SALERIO

I would it might prove the end of his losses.   15

SOLANIO

Let me say "amen"[10] betimes,[11] lest the devil cross my prayer,
for here he comes in the likeness of a Jew.

12 *the wings*. Salerio is referring to the page's clothes which Jessica was wearing when she escaped with Lorenzo. He calls them *wings* so as to make fun of Shylock's word *flight*, "secret escape", and Solanio continues the joke with *bird* and *fledged* in line 23 below.

13 *fledged* – "ready to fly away".

14 *complexion* – "natural inclination".

15 *dam* – "mother (bird)". Shylock now plays on the word; he uses *damned* in the next line.

16 *the devil*. Salerio is referring to Shylock; cf. lines 16 and 17 above.

17 *My own … blood* – "my own child".

18 *old carrion*. This is an abusive name; *carrion* means flesh, and Solanio suggests that Shylock, in saying "My own flesh and blood to rebel!" is referring to desires of the flesh. Solanio asks him, "Does it (your fleshly desire) get out of control (*rebels it*) at your age?" Shylock explains what he meant in the following line.

19 *jet and ivory* represent a contrast between the very black and the very white.

20 *Rhenish*, a white wine from the district of the River Rhine.

Enter SHYLOCK

How now, Shylock! what news among the merchants?

SHYLOCK

You knew, none so well, none so well as you, of my daughter's
flight.   *he feels mocked*   20

SALERIO

That 's certain; I, for my part, knew the tailor that made the
wings[12] she flew withal.

SOLANIO

And Shylock, for his own part, knew the bird was fledged,[13]
and then it is the complexion[14] of them all to leave the dam.[15]

SHYLOCK

She is damned for it.   25

SALERIO

That 's certain, if the devil[16] may be her judge.

SHYLOCK

My own[17] flesh and blood to rebel!

SOLANIO

Out upon it, old carrion![18] rebels it at these years?   *misinterpretation*

SHYLOCK

I say my daughter is my flesh and my blood.

SALERIO

There is more difference between thy flesh and hers than   30
between jet and ivory,[19] more between your bloods than
there is between red wine and Rhenish.[20] But tell us, do you
hear whether Antonio have had any loss at sea or no?

21 *match* – "bargain", and perhaps also with the idea of someone he is "matched against", i.e. in contest with, over some arrangement. In this second sense his daughter was a *bad match*, since he has lost her, and Antonio may become another, since he may not be able to pay back the money he has borrowed.

22 *was used to* – "used to".

23 *come so ... mart* – "come on to the market-place (the Rialto) looking so smart and pleased with himself".

24 *for a Christian courtesy* – "as a Christian act of kindness", not charging interest; Shylock has objected to this before (1.iii.37–8).

25 *if he forfeit* – "if he has to pay the penalty".

26 *To bait fish withal* – "To use as a bait for catching fish". Now follows one of Shylock's great speeches. Against him, it becomes clear that he hates Antonio because Antonio is good and generous; for him, what he says of his own humanity is nothing but the truth: he is a human being in every sense that a Christian is.

27 *hindered ... million* – "prevented me from making a profit of half a million ducats", apparently by lending money free of interest to borrowers who would otherwise have had to pay interest to Shylock.

28 *dimensions* – "a bodily frame".

29 *affections* – "desires".

30 *what is his humility?* – "what sort of gentleness (*humility*) does he (the Christian) show?" Shylock seems to use *humility* to mean "gentleness of mind, patience", but there is also a reference to humility (in the modern English sense) as being the characteristic Christian virtue.

31 *his sufferance* – "his (the Jew's) patient suffering". *Sufferance* here means submitting to ill-treatment without complaint. Shylock is speaking ironically: the revenge he talks of is not in the least according to Christian humility, and it is just the opposite of *sufferance*.

32 *it shall ... instruction* – "things will be very hard against me if I do not do better (in exercising revenge) than those who instruct me". He is now pretending that he has learnt how to get revenge by watching the behaviour of Christians, who in this sense have "instructed" him in it.

– common humanity

old testament

barbarian
(lack of civilisation

new testament.
civilised

Revenge = primal drives

common humanity

106

SHYLOCK

There I have another bad match,[21] a bankrupt, a prodigal, who dare scarce show his head on the Rialto, a beggar that was used to[22] come so[23] smug upon the mart. Let him look to his bond! He was wont to call me usurer; let him look to his bond! He was wont to lend money for a Christian courtesy;[24] let him look to his bond! 35

SALERIO

Why, I am sure, if he forfeit,[25] thou wilt not take his flesh – what's *that* good for? 40

SHYLOCK

To bait fish withal;[26] – if it will feed nothing else, it will feed my revenge. He hath disgraced me, and hindered[27] me half a million – laughed at my losses, mocked at my gains, scorned my nation, thwarted my bargains, cooled my friends, heated mine enemies – and what's his reason? I am a Jew. Hath not a Jew eyes? hath not a Jew hands, organs, dimensions,[28] senses, affections,[29] passions? fed with the same food, hurt with the same weapons, subject to the same diseases, healed by the same means, warmed and cooled by the same winter and summer as a Christian is? If you prick us, do we not bleed? if you tickle us, do we not laugh? if you poison us, do we not die? – And if you wrong us, shall we not revenge? If we are like you in the rest, we will resemble you in that. If a Jew wrong a Christian, what is his humility?[30] Revenge! If a Christian wrong a Jew, what should his sufferance[31] be by Christian example? Why, revenge! The villainy you teach me I will execute, and it shall[32] go hard but I will better the instruction. 45 50 55

Enter a Serving-man *from* ANTONIO

SERVING-MAN

Gentlemen, my master Antonio is at his house, and desires to speak with you both. 60

33 *Tubal*, a Jewish friend of Shylock's, has been out looking for Jessica, but so far without success.

34 *a third . . . matched* – "a third cannot be found to compare with them".

35 *A diamond gone* – "One of the diamonds which went"; it was taken by Jessica.

36 *hearsed* – "placed in a coffin".

37 *thou*. One of the early editions of the play reads *then* for *thou*, which makes good sense. But perhaps Shylock is simply beginning a sentence which he does not finish because his anger drives him quickly from one point to another. It is clear that his losses in property are now uppermost in his mind; the flight of his daughter has taken second place.

38 *so much . . . so much* – "so much money", the cost of the search for his daughter.

39 *nor no ill . . . shoulders* – "and no bad luck about (*stirring*, 'on the move') except what comes down (*lights*) on *my* shoulders", i.e. what *I* have to bear.

SALERIO

We have been up and down to seek him.

Enter TUBAL[33]

SOLANIO

Here comes another of the tribe; a third[34] cannot be matched
unless the devil himself turn Jew.

[*Exeunt* SOLANIO *and* SALERIO *with the* Serving-man

SHYLOCK

How now, Tubal! what news from Genoa? has thou found   65
my daughter?

TUBAL

I often came where I did hear of her, but cannot find her.

money / covered SHYLOCK

Why there, there, there, there! A diamond gone[35] cost me
two thousand ducats in Frankfort – the curse never fell upon
our nation till now, I never felt it till now – two thousand   70
ducats in that and other precious, precious jewels. I would my
daughter were dead at my foot, and the jewels in her ear;
would she were hearsed[36] at my foot, and the ducats in her
coffin. – No news of them? why, so! – and I know not what's
spent in the search: why thou[37] – loss upon loss! The thief gone   75
with so much,[38] and so much to find the thief, and no satisfac-
tion, no revenge, nor no ill[39] luck stirring but what lights on *my*
shoulders, no sighs but of *my* breathing, no tears but of *my*
shedding.   *revenge*
                                                        in humiliation

TUBAL

Yes, other men have ill luck too – Antonio, as I heard in   80
Genoa, –

SHYLOCK

What, what, what? ill luck, ill luck?

40 *cast away* – "lost, wrecked".

41 *Tripolis* – Tripoli, in North Africa.

42 *heard in Genoa*. For *heard* the earliest editions of the play give *heere* – "here", which does not make good sense. It is most likely that Shylock is here simply going over the points he has heard from Tubal, and repeating the source of the information, "as I heard in Genoa" (lines 80–1).

43 *one night* – "in one night".

44 *fourscore* – "eighty", i.e. four times twenty.

45 *at a sitting* – "on one occasion".

46 *divers* – "a number".

47 *he cannot … break* – "he has no alternative but to go bankrupt (*break*)".

48 *had of* – "got from".

49 *Out upon her!* – "Curse her!"

50 *I had it of Leah* – "it was a present from Leah" (his wife).

Jessica's alertment enhance the revenge Justifying

TUBAL

– hath an argosy cast away[40] coming from Tripolis.[41]

SHYLOCK

I thank God, I thank God! Is it true, is it true?

TUBAL

I spoke with some of the sailors that escaped the wreck.   85

SHYLOCK

I thank thee, good Tubal; good news, good news: ha ha! heard[42] in Genoa!

TUBAL

Your daughter spent in Genoa, as I heard, one night,[43] fourscore[44] ducats.

SHYLOCK

Thou stick'st a dagger in me – I shall never see my gold again –   90
fourscore ducats at a sitting,[45] fourscore ducats!

TUBAL

There came divers[46] of Antonio's creditors in my company to Venice, that swear he cannot[47] choose but break.

SHYLOCK

I am very glad of it – I'll plague him, I'll torture him – I am glad of it.   95

TUBAL

One of them showed me a ring that he had of[48] your daughter for a monkey.

SHYLOCK

Out upon her![49] – Thou torturest me, Tubal – it was my turquoise; I had it of Leah[50] when I was a bachelor. I would not have given it for a wilderness of monkeys.   100

III

51 *undone* – "ruined". Tubal has, in one sense, "played" with Shylock. He tells him bad news, and then reminds him that he has some hope of revenge on Antonio (ll. 80-3, 92-3); then he gives more bad news, of Jessica spending money freely in Genoa (88-9), and Shylock reacts accordingly; again he reminds Shylock of Antonio's misfortunes (101), and then of Shylock's own, and so on. Each time, Shylock moves with him, swinging from anger to devilish pleasure and back again.

52 *fee me . . . before* – "hire a sheriff's officer for me; arrange for him to be available (*bespeak him*) a fortnight before (Antonio's debt is to be repaid)". The duty of the sheriff's officer was to arrest wrong-doers on the sheriff's orders.

53 *for were he . . . will* – "for if he (Antonio) is out of Venice I can drive whatever bargains (*merchandise*) I wish". Antonio's kindheartedness in business will no longer affect trading and moneylending in Venice.

(III.ii) In this scene Bassanio wins the hand of Portia in marriage. The wooing and the choosing of the caskets are an occasion for long speeches in a rather formal, courtly style which seems to be more concerned with balanced phrases and plays on words than with the expression of real feeling. But that was the custom of the time; and there are places where passion is clearly expressed, as when Portia hesitates during her first speech (lines 7 ff.), and when Bassanio, having won his suit, compares himself with a champion who has won a fight and is dizzily enjoying the applause of the audience (lines 141 ff.).

Portia shows that Bassanio is the man she truly loves; she tries to persuade him to delay in choosing the caskets so that she will certainly have more of his company, but he wants to choose at once. To Portia's delight he chooses the lead casket, and finds her picture inside, and a verse which shows that his reasoning was correct: he was not deceived by outward appearances. Gratiano tells how he, too, has fallen in love and intends to marry Portia's maid Nerissa.

Lorenzo, Jessica, and Salerio break in on this happy scene to bring Bassanio a letter from Antonio. From the letter they learn that Antonio has had bad luck with his ships and will not be able to pay back his loan in time. He fears he will have to pay the forfeit, which means death, and asks only that Bassanio should see him before he has to die. Portia thinks the loan very small and offers to pay many times the amount. First, she says, Bassanio and she must marry, and then Bassanio must go off to help his friend.

1 *hazard* – "make a choice (of the caskets)".

continued on page 114

TUBAL

But Antonio is certainly undone.[51]

SHYLOCK

Nay, that 's true, that 's very true. – Go, Tubal, fee me[52]
an officer, bespeak him a fortnight before – I will have the
heart of him if he forfeit, for were he[53] out of Venice I can
make what merchandise I will. Go, Tubal, and meet me at 105
our synagogue – go, good Tubal – at our synagogue, Tubal.

cumunity

[*Exeunt*

Scene II. Belmont. A room in Portia's house.

Enter BASSANIO, PORTIA, GRATIANO, NERISSA,
and all their trains.

PORTIA

I pray you, tarry; pause a day or two
Before you hazard,[1] for in choosing wrong
I lose your company; therefore forbear a while.
There 's something tells me – but it is not love[2] –
I would not lose you; and you know yourself,   5
Hate counsels[3] not in such a quality.
But lest you should not understand me well –
And yet[4] a maiden hath no tongue but thought –
I would detain you here some month or two[5]
Before you venture[6] for me. I could teach you   10
How to choose right, but then I am forsworn;[7]
So will[8] I never be; so may you miss me;
But if you do, you 'll make me wish a sin,
That I had been forsworn. Beshrew[9] your eyes;
They have o'erlooked me[10] and divided me;   15
One half of me[11] is yours, the other half yours –
Mine own I would say; but if mine, then yours,
And so all yours. O, these naughty[12] times

2 *it is not love.* Portia is being very careful in what she says, since she does not wish anyone to think that she favours one suitor above another. But her guarded talk does not last for long, and by the end of her speech it is clear that Bassanio is the man she really loves.

3 *Hate counsels . . . quality* – "It is not *hate* which advises you in this way (*quality*)". It is, on the contrary, *love* which makes her ask him to stay.

4 *And yet . . . thought.* Portia probably means that it is more proper for an unmarried woman to think her thoughts than to speak them out aloud. But she is obviously moved by her love, and does not speak very clearly.

5 *some month or two . . .*; a moment ago she was begging for just a *day or two* (line 1).

6 *venture* – "try your luck". The word reminds us of the business ventures of the merchants of Venice.

7 *I am forsworn* – "I would be breaking my promise".

8 *So will . . . miss me* – "I shall never be like this (i.e. *forsworn*, not keeping my word), and so it is possible that you may lose me".

9 *Beshrew* – "May evil befall".

10 *o'erlooked me* – "looked on me with the 'evil eye'". This talk is light-hearted, and not to be understood literally. Portia is saying in a number of ways that she has fallen in love with Bassanio.

11 *One half of me . . .* This strange way of expressing her feelings is in keeping with Portia's wish not to speak openly of her love. It is in fact a play of words on the idea *divide* (line 15), and comparable to that on *forsworn* in lines 11 ff. Bassanio's look has bewitched her and split her personality: of the two halves, it would be a pattern of speech to say that one was hers and one his – but *all* is his if she is free to give her hand.

12 *naughty* – "bad".

13 *though yours, not yours* – "though yours by right, not yours in fact", because there is a *bar* between the owner and the rights.

14 *Prove it so* – "If it should prove so", i.e. that Portia does not become Bassanio's in fact.

15 *not I* (go to hell), i.e. for the sin of breaking my promise.

16 *peize.* This word is usually explained as meaning "weigh down" – "to weigh down the time so as to make it pass slowly". But it is more likely to be a form of *piece*, and to mean "piece out, extend", and therefore to link with *eche* in the following line.

17 *eche* – (probably pronounced as the modern English word *each*) is a form of *eke* – "add to, increase".

18 *stay* – "keep".

19 *election* – "choice (of the caskets)".

20 *treason.* The rack, an instrument of torture, was once used to make traitors confess their treason. *Rack* thus links with *treason*, and this imagery is extended in the following lines.

21 *fear* – "doubt". He doubts whether he will ever be able to enjoy his love.

22 *enforcéd* – "made to act by compulsion".

23 *Had been the very sum* – "would have been the absolute total".

Put bars between the owners and their rights!
And so though yours, not yours.[13] Prove it so,[14]   20
Let Fortune go to hell for it, not I.[15]
I speak too long, but 't is to peize[16] the time,
To eche[17] it, and to draw it out in length,
To stay[18] you from election.[19]

BASSANIO

     Let me choose,
For as I am, I live upon the rack.   25

PORTIA

Upon the rack, Bassanio? then confess
What treason[20] there is mingled with your love.

BASSANIO

None but that ugly treason of mistrust,
Which makes me fear[21] th' enjoying of my love.
There may as well be amity and life   30
'Tween snow and fire, as treason and my love.

PORTIA

Ay, but I fear you speak upon the rack
Where men enforcéd[22] do speak anything.

BASSANIO

Promise me life, and I 'll confess the truth.

PORTIA

Well then, confess and live.

BASSANIO

     "Confess and love"   35
Had been the very sum[23] of my confession.
O happy torment, when my torturer

24 *answers for deliverance* – "answers which will deliver me (from the rack)". The torture was stopped if the sufferer answered in the way the torturer wished.

25 *a swan-like end.* The commonest type of swan has no cry, but it was said that swans sang shortly before they were going to die. If Bassanio is to "die", i.e. lose the love he so deeply feels, then, like the swan, he is to "fade in music". This image is extended in the following lines.

26 *That the comparison ... proper* – "So that the image (*comparison*, the music and a swan-song) may be more firmly established"; the imagery is now made to include the stream on which the swan is swimming.

27 *Even as* – "just like".

28 *dulcet* – "sweet". The *dulcet sounds* were music played beneath a bridegroom's window on his wedding morning.

29 *With no less ... love; presence* – "nobleness". In a classical story, Hesione, the daughter of Laomedon, King of Troy, was bound to a rock as an offering (*The virgin tribute* of line 56) demanded by a sea monster. Hercules (called *Alcides* in line 55) promised to save her, not for love, but for the reward her father had promised; this was the horses given him by the god Zeus.

30 *Troy*, i.e. the King of Troy.

31 *stand for* – "represent".

32 *The rest aloof* – "the other people, standing aside", as Portia had ordered them to do in line 42.

33 *Dardanian* – "Trojan, of Troy".

34 *With blearéd visages* – "who, with faces marked by weeping". *Blearéd* means "made dull with weeping".

35 *issue* – "result".

36 *Live thou* – "If you live".

37 *fray* – "contest, battle".

38 *A song.* Some have thought that this song gives Bassanio a clue to the riddle of the caskets. It tells of the death of *Fancy* – "attraction not founded on reason; foolish affection". *Fancy* is felt through the eyes, not the heart, and this suggests that the song recommends Bassanio not to choose on the strength of outward appearances. Again, it has been pointed out that the lines of the first part of the song end in words which rhyme with *lead*, the metal of which the winning casket is made.

But against this, Bassanio is clearly commenting to himself on the caskets while the song is being sung (so the stage direction demands), and cannot be expected to hear it or learn its message. And Portia is bound not to help the suitors in their choice; she said,

I could teach you
How to choose right, but then I am forsworn;
So will I never be (lines 10–12 above).

However, the song has a message which is in agreement with Bassanio's reasoning, as can be seen in his next speech.

39 *Or ... or* – "either ... or".

40 *begot* – "conceived".

41 *Reply, reply.* In the earliest editions these words are printed on the right-hand side of the column following the first three lines of the song. It is assumed that all sing them as a refrain (as they do the last line), dividing the question from the answer.

42 *engendered* – "conceived", and parallel to *begot* in the question; so *fed* in the following line is parallel to *nourishéd*.

Doth teach me answers for deliverance ![24]
But let me to my fortune and the caskets.

PORTIA

Away then! I am locked in one of them;   40
If you do love me, you will find me out.
Nerissa and the rest, stand all aloof!
Let music sound while he doth make his choice;
Then if he lose he makes a swan-like end,[25]
Fading in music. That the comparison[26]   45
May stand more proper, my eye shall be the stream
And wat'ry death-bed for him. He may win,
And what is music then? Then music is
Even as[27] the flourish, when true subjects bow
To a new-crownéd monarch; such it is,   50
As are those dulcet[28] sounds in break of day
That creep into the dreaming bridegroom's ear,
And summon him to marriage. Now he goes,
With no less[29] presence, but with much more love,
Than young Alcides, when he did redeem   55
The virgin tribute, paid by howling Troy[30]
To the sea-monster. I stand for[31] sacrifice;
The rest aloof[32] are the Dardanian[33] wives,
With blearéd visages[34] come forth to view
The issue[35] of th' exploit. Go, Hercules!   60
Live thou,[36] I live; with much, much more dismay,
I view the fight, than thou that mak'st the fray.[37]

A song[38] to music whilst BASSANIO *comments on the
caskets to himself.*

   Tell me where is Fancy bred,
   Or[39] in the heart, or in the head?
   How begot,[40] how nourishéd?   65

All. *Reply, reply.*[41]

   It is engendered[42] in the eyes,

43 *In the cradle*, i.e. when it is very young. *Fancy* cannot live long without deeper love.

44 *knell*, the bell rung when someone is dying.

45 *So may the outward shows ...* Bassanio's comments show that he has been thinking on the same lines as the message of the song: outward show is not to be trusted; the eye must not be allowed to deceive the heart. Certainly Portia has faith that the lottery will get her the right husband: she said (line 41).

   If you do love me, you will find me out.

46 *The world* – "people in general".

47 *still* – "continually".

48 *ornament* – "outward show".

49 *what plea ... But ... Obscures* (line 77) – "what plea is there ... which does not obscure"; i.e. there is no plea at all which, if made in a pleasant way, makes the case look better than it really is. The question asked in the text is assumed to be answered by "None".

50 *What damnéd error but ... bless it* – "What mistake worthy of damnation is there which some serious thinker (*sober brow*) will not bless".

51 *approve it with a text* – "quote a text (from the Bible) to confirm his approval of it".

52 *the grossness* – "the wickedness (of error)".

53 *so simple, but assumes* – "so plain that it does not assume".

54 *The beards of Hercules ... Mars.* A man's strength was sometimes shown by his hair; a good beard, therefore, indicated a brave, strong man. Mars was the Roman god of war, thought of here as bearded and frowning.

55 *inward searched* – "if examined within".

56 *livers white as milk*. A pale, white liver was thought of as a sign of cowardice.

57 *but valour's excrement* – "only the outward growth of valour".

58 *To render them redoubted* – "to make them look terrible (to an enemy)".

59 *'t is purchased ... weight* – "it is bought at so much money an ounce". This refers to cosmetics, preparations which women use to add beauty to the face. Again this is, of course, only outward beauty, not beauty of the soul.

60 *lightest*: this plays on (1) *light* as the opposite of *heavy*, and (2) (of a woman) "somewhat immoral". The *miracle* (line 90) is that the thing which adds to the weight (the cosmetic) should yet make "lighter".

61 *crispéd* – "curled".

62 *Upon supposéd fairness* – "worn by those who appear beautiful (but are not really so)".

63 *dowry* – "gift at death, endowment".

64 *sepulchre* – "grave". The hair described here is false; it is taken from one head and made to be worn by someone else.

65 *guiléd* – "deceiving, treacherous".

66 *the beauteous ... beauty*. This phrase has not been satisfactorily explained, and the wording may not be as Shakespeare wrote it – it is unusual to have two such words as *beauteous* and *beauty* so close together. Possibly, in the England of Shakespeare's day, an Indian beauty (who would be thought of as dark-skinned) was not considered a beauty at all.

> With gazing fed, and Fancy dies
> In the cradle[43] where it lies.
> Let us all ring Fancy's knell;[44]   70
> I'll begin it, – Ding, dong, bell.

All. *Ding, dong, bell.*

BASSANIO

So may the outward shows[45] be least themselves;
The world[46] is still[47] deceived with ornament.[48]
In law, what plea[49] so tainted and corrupt,   75
But, being seasoned with a gracious voice,
Obscures the show of evil? In religion,
What damnéd error but[50] some sober brow
Will bless it, and approve it with a text,[51]
Hiding the grossness[52] with fair ornament?   80
There is no vice so simple, but assumes[53]
Some mark of virtue on his outward parts.
How many cowards whose hearts are all as false
As stairs of sand, wear yet upon their chins
The beards of Hercules[54] and frowning Mars,   85
Who, inward searched,[55] have livers white as milk?[56]
And these assume but valour's excrement[57]
To render them redoubted.[58] Look on beauty,
And you shall see 't is purchased[59] by the weight,
Which therein works a miracle in nature,   90
Making them lightest[60] that wear most of it;
So are those crispéd,[61] snaky golden locks
Which make such wanton gambols with the wind
Upon supposéd fairness,[62] often known
To be the dowry[63] of a second head,   95
The skull that bred them in the sepulchre.[64]
Thus ornament is but the guiléd[65] shore
To a most dangerous sea, the beauteous[66] scarf
Veiling an Indian beauty – in a word,
The seeming truth which cunning times put on   100
To entrap the wisest. Therefore, thou gaudy gold,

67 *Midas*, a King of Phrygia in Asia Minor, was very rich, but wanted still more gold. As a reward for a kindness he did, he asked that everything he touched should turn to gold. His wish was granted, but because even the food and drink he touched turned to gold he begged the god Dionysus to take back the gift.

68 *drudge 'Tween man and man*, i.e. the silver of the second casket; silver is the metal from which coins are made, and money is a "common servant" (*drudge*) passing between one man and another.

69 *paleness*. This is the word used here in all the early editions of the play; but, because *pale* has already been used of the silver (line 103), many have thought that it is a mistake for another word such as *plainness*. But if *Thy* is stressed (as in the text here), a sufficient contrast is made. Again, *eloquence* was sometimes called *coloured* in contrast to *plain*-speaking. The line can then be explained: "*Your* plain-speaking has a greater effect on me than (coloured) eloquence".

70 *fleet to air* – "fly away, disappear in the air".

71 *As* – "such as".

72 *rash-embraced despair* – "despair assumed too quickly".

73 *In measure* – "in moderation, not too abundantly".

74 *scant* – "restrain".

75 *For fear I surfeit* – "in case I take too much".

76 *counterfeit* – "picture".

77 *come so near creation*, i.e. made a picture which is so like the real thing. To do this the painter must have been a demi-god, since he almost created something.

78 *Or whether* – "or".

79 *the balls of mine* – "my own eye-balls".

80 *plays*, i.e. plays the part of.

81 *Faster* – "more firmly".

82 *unfurnished* – "without a mate", i.e. without the other eye.

83 *substance . . . shadow*. Bassanio plays on these words: the *substance* is the original (Portia) of which the *shadow* is the picture, but *substance* in this line means "subject".

84 *underprizing* – "undervaluing".

85 *The continent and summary* – "that which contains and sums up".

Hard food for Midas,[67] ~~I will none of thee,~~
Nor none of thee, thou pale and common drudge
'Tween man and man.[68] But thou, thou meagre lead,
Which rather threaten'st than dost promise aught,   105
Thy paleness[69] moves me more than eloquence,
And here choose I; joy be the consequence!

PORTIA

[*Aside*] How all the other passions fleet to air,[70]
As[71] doubtful thoughts, and rash-embraced despair,[72]
And shudd'ring fear, and green-eyed jealousy.   110
O love, be moderate, allay thy ecstasy!
In measure[73] rain thy joy, scant[74] this excess!
I feel too much thy blessing; make it less
For fear I surfeit![75]

BASSANIO

What find I here?

[*He opens the lead casket*

Fair Portia's counterfeit![76] What demi-god   115
Hath come so near creation?[77] Move these eyes?
Or whether[78] (riding on the balls of mine)[79]
Seem they in motion? Here are severed lips
Parted with sugar breath; so sweet a bar
Should sunder such sweet friends. Here in her hairs   120
The painter plays[80] the spider, and hath woven
A golden mesh t' entrap the hearts of men
Faster[81] than gnats in cobwebs. But her eyes!
How could he see to do them? having made one,
Methinks it should have power to steal both his   125
And leave itself unfurnished.[82] Yet look how far
The substance[83] of my praise doth wrong this shadow
In underprizing[84] it, so far this shadow
Doth limp behind the substance. Here's the scroll,
The continent and summary[85] of my fortune.   130

86 *by the view* – "by outward appearances".

87 *new*, i.e. new fortune.

88 *hold your . . . bliss* – "consider your luck (*fortune*) to be your happiness".

89 *by note* – "in accordance with the 'bill', or *note* of what is due to me", i.e. a kiss exchanged between them.

90 *prize* – "contest".

91 *livings* – "property".

92 *sum of* – *something*. Perhaps Portia is thinking of the phrase *sum of all* – "sum total", but hesitates before *all* and changes it to *something* so as not to sound too boastful. But perhaps the text is faulty here.

93 *to term in gross* – "to give as a sum total".

94 *bred* – "brought up".

> *You that choose not by the view,*[86]
> *Chance as fair, and choose as true!*
> *Since this fortune falls to you,*
> *Be content, and seek no new.*[87]
> *If you be well pleased with this,*   135
> *And hold your fortune for your bliss,*[88]
> *Turn you where your lady is,*
> *And claim her with a loving kiss.*

A gentle scroll. Fair lady, by your leave,
I come by note[89] to give, and to receive.   140
[*He kisses her*] Like one of two contending in a prize[90]
That thinks he hath done well in people's eyes,
Hearing applause and universal shout,
Giddy in spirit, still gazing in a doubt
Whether those peals of praise be his or no,   145
So, thrice-fair lady, stand I even so,
As doubtful whether what I see be true,
Until confirmed, signed, ratified by you.

PORTIA

You see me, Lord Bassanio, where I stand,
Such as I am; though for myself alone
I would not be ambitious in my wish
To wish myself much better, yet for you,
I would be trebled twenty times myself,
A thousand times more fair, ten thousand times more rich,
That only to stand high in your account,   155
I might in virtues, beauties, livings,[91] friends
Exceed account. But the full sum of me
Is sum of – something:[92] which, to term in gross,[93]
Is an unlessoned girl, unschooled, unpractised;
Happy in this, she is not yet so old   160
But she may learn; happier than this,
She is not bred[94] so dull but she can learn;
Happiest of all, is that her gentle spirit

123

95 *converted* – "given over".
96 *But now* – "Just now, a moment ago".
97 *even now, but now* – "at this very moment".
98 *my vantage . . . you* – "my opportunity to accuse you aloud".
99 *fairly spoke* – "beautifully spoken".
100 *every something . . . together* – "everything (all the noise from the crowd) being blended together".
101 *wild* – literally "wilderness", a "waste of sound" without recognizable features.

102 *save of* – "except".
103 *you can . . . me*; since they have all the joy they could wish for in one another, Gratiano has no more to wish them.
104 *your honours*, a polite way of saying "you".
105 *mean to . . . faith* – "intend to perform correctly (*solemnize*) the exchange of your promises", i.e. get married in church.

this fair mansion

Commits itself to yours to be directed,
As from her lord, her governor, her king.   165
Myself, and what is mine, to you and yours
Is now converted.[95] But now[96] I was the lord
Of this fair mansion, master of my servants,
Queen o'er myself; and even now, but now,[97]
This house, these servants, and this same myself   170
Are yours, my lord! I give them with this ring,
Which when you part from, lose, or give away,
Let it presage the ruin of your love,
And be my vantage[98] to exclaim on you.

BASSANIO

Madam, you have bereft me of all words;   *foreshadowing* 175
Only my blood speaks to you in my veins,
And there is such confusion in my powers,
As after some oration fairly spoke[99]
By a belovéd prince, there doth appear
Among the buzzing pleaséd multitude –   180
Where every something[100] being blent together,
Turns to a wild[101] of nothing, save of[102] joy
Expressed, and not expressed. But when this ring
Parts from this finger, then parts life from hence; –
O, then be bold to say Bassanio 's dead!   185

NERISSA

My lord and lady, it is now our time
That have stood by and seen our wishes prosper,
To cry "good joy". Good joy, my lord and lady!

GRATIANO

My lord Bassanio, and my gentle lady,
I wish you all the joy that *you* can[103] wish;   190
For I am sure you can wish none from me.
And when your honours[104] mean to[105] solemnize

106 *so* – "so long as".

107 *swift* – "swiftly, quickly".

108 *for intermission ... you* – "for there is no more delay (*intermission*) in my case than in yours, my lord". He means that he has won a wife as quickly as Bassanio.

109 *as the matter falls* – "as it happens".

110 *until I sweat again* – "until it makes me sweat", i.e., most vigorously.

111 *roof*, i.e. roof or top of his mouth.

112 *of* – "from".

113 *so you ... withal* – "if you are pleased with it (the match)".

Virtue
|
fitting of social order
Bassanio - Portio.
Gratiano - Nerissa
Belmont = virtuous and more cultured / civilise
influence

The bargain of your faith, I do beseech you
Even at that time I may be married too.

BASSANIO

With all my heart, so[106] thou canst get a wife.   195

GRATIANO

I thank your lordship, you have got me one.
My eyes, my lord, can look as swift[107] as yours:
You saw the mistress, I beheld the maid;
You loved, I loved; – for intermission[108]
No more pertains to me, my lord, than you.   200
Your fortune stood upon the caskets there,
And so did mine too, as the matter falls;[109]
For wooing here until I sweat again,[110]
And swearing till my very roof[111] was dry
With oaths of love, at last, if promise last,   205
I got a promise of[112] this fair one here
To have her love, provided that your fortune
Achieved her mistress.

PORTIA

Is this true, Nerissa?

NERISSA

Madam, it is, so you[113] stand pleased withal.

BASSANIO

And do you, Gratiano, mean good faith?   210

GRATIANO

Yes, faith, my lord.

BASSANIO

Our feast shall be much honoured in your marriage.

114 *We'll play . . . thousand ducats*, i.e. whoever has the first boy will get a thousand ducats from the other couple.

115 *stake*, i.e. the thousand ducats, which are to be put down for the contest.

116 *If that . . . welcome* – "if I have the right (*power*) to bid you welcome despite the newness (*youth*) of my possession (*interest*) here". By winning Portia he has just won her house and property.

117 *very* – "true".

118 *My purpose was not* – "it was not my plan".

119 *past all saying nay* – "beyond all refusal"; *nay* – "no".

120 *him* – "himself". He "sends greetings".

Flesh ⟷ price.

GRATIANO

We 'll play[114] with them the first boy for a thousand ducats.

NERISSA

What! and stake[115] down?

GRATIANO

No, we shall ne'er win at that sport and stake down. *II* 215
But who comes here? Lorenzo and his infidel! *untrue*
What! and my old Venetian friend Salerio?

infidelity

outsider.

Enter LORENZO, JESSICA, *and* SALERIO.

Subhuman.

BASSANIO

Lorenzo and Salerio, welcome hither,
If that the youth[116] of my new int'rest here
Have power to bid you welcome. By your leave
I bid my very[117] friends and countrymen,   220
Sweet Portia, welcome.

presumption

PORTIA

So do I my lord;
They are entirely welcome.

LORENZO

I thank your honour. – For my part, my lord,
My purpose was not[118] to have seen you here,   225
But meeting with Salerio by the way,
He did entreat me, past all saying nay,[119]
To come with him along.

SALERIO

I did, my lord,
And I have reason for it. Signior Antonio
Commends him[120] to you.   [*He gives* BASSANIO *a letter*

121 *Ere I ope* – "Before I open".

122 *doth* – "is, fares".

123 *Not sick ... in mind* (line 233). Salerio seems to mean that Antonio is well in body but his ills and their remedy lie in his mind; there his troubles are, and there he will have to look for comfort.

124 *estate* – "condition".

125 *cheer yon stranger* – "welcome that stranger over there".

126 *royal merchant* – "king of merchants", i.e. richest, most important; he was not, of course, really *royal*, i.e. of a royal family.

127 *We are ... fleece.* In a Greek legend, Jason, the son of King Aeson, lost his father's kingdom to his half-brother, and to get it back had to bring a golden fleece which was guarded by a dragon. He and other Greek heroes set sail in the ship *Argo*, and eventually won the fleece. The heroes were called the Argonauts, and Gratiano's mention of the legend may be partly a play upon the words *Argonauts* and *argosies,* the name given to Antonio's ships (as at I.i.9). The story was mentioned earlier in the play by Bassanio (*v.* I.i.168-171; note 81, p. 12; and p. xi of the Introduction).

128 *fleece* is perhaps a play on *fleets* – "many ships".

129 *shrewd* – "evil".

130 *That steals* – "which steal".

131 *turn ... the constitution* – "change the look (on the face)".

132 *constant* – "healthy, balanced".

133 *With leave* – "Please". As Bassanio looks more and more worried, Portia becomes more and more anxious to know what bad news there is in the letter.

BASSANIO

Ere I ope[121] his letter,   230
I pray you tell me how my good friend doth.[122]

SALERIO

Not sick,[123] my lord, unless it be in mind,
Nor well, unless in mind; his letter there
Will show you his estate.[124]   [BASSANIO *opens the letter*

GRATIANO

Nerissa, cheer yon stranger,[125] bid her welcome.   235
Your hand, Salerio [*They shake hands*] what 's the news from
    Venice?
How doth that royal merchant,[126] good Antonio?
I know he will be glad of our success;
We are[127] the Jasons, we have won the fleece.

SALERIO

I would you had won the fleece[128] that he hath lost.   240

PORTIA

There are some shrewd[129] contents in yon same paper,
That steals[130] the colour from Bassanio's cheek –
Some dear friend dead, else nothing in the world
Could turn[131] so much the constitution
Of any constant[132] man. What, worse and worse?   245
With leave,[133] Bassanio, I am half yourself,
And I must freely have the half of anything
That this same paper brings you.

BASSANIO

                              O sweet Portia,
Here are a few of the unpleasant'st words
That ever blotted paper ! Gentle lady,   250
When I did first impart my love to you,

131

134 *all the wealth . . . veins*, i.e. he had no property, but his blood, his family, was good.

135 *Rating myself . . . braggart.* He boasted (was a *braggart*) even when he said he had nothing, for in fact he had less than nothing; he was in debt to a friend, and this friend has now had bad luck.

136 *engaged myself to* – "put myself in the hands of".

137 *mere* – "absolute". Antonio's *mere enemy* is, of course, Shylock.

138 *feed my means* – "get supplies of money".

139 *as* – "is like".

140 *hit* – "been successful".

141 *scape* – "escaped".

142 *it should appear* – "it seems".

143 *The present money . . . the Jew* – "the money available (*present*) to pay what he owes the Jew".

144 *keen* – "cruel".

145 *confound* – "bring to ruin".

146 *plies* – "strongly attacks (with requests, questions, etc.)".

147 *doth impeach . . . state* – "calls in question the reputation of the state for giving everyone equal rights in the eyes of the law"; i.e. Shylock is going about saying that if his case is not treated properly he will bring discredit on that justice which is supposed to be the right of everyone in Venice.

148 *magnificoes* – "chief men (of Venice)".

149 *port* – "dignity".

150 *persuaded* – "pleaded".

151 *envious* – "evil".

I freely told you all the wealth[134] I had
Ran in my veins – I was a gentleman;
And then I told you true. And yet, dear lady,
Rating myself[135] at nothing, you shall see   255
How much I was a braggart. – When I told you
My state was nothing, I should then have told you
That I was worse than nothing; for indeed
I have engaged myself to[136] a dear friend,
Engaged my friend to his mere[137] enemy   260
To feed my means.[138] Here is a letter, lady;
The paper as[139] the body of my friend,
And every word in it a gaping wound
Issuing life-blood. But is it true, Salerio?
Hath *all* his ventures failed? what, not *one* hit?[140]   265
From Tripolis, from Mexico, and England,
From Lisbon, Barbary, and India,
And not one vessel scape[141] the dreadful touch
Of merchant-marring rocks?

SALERIO

Not one, my lord.

Besides, it should appear[142] that if he had   270
The present[143] money to discharge the Jew,
He would not take it. Never did I know
A creature that did bear the shape of man
So keen[144] and greedy to confound[145] a man.
He plies[146] the duke at morning and at night,   275
And doth impeach[147] the freedom of the state
If they deny him justice. Twenty merchants,
The duke himself, and the magnificoes[148]
Of greatest port[149] have all persuaded[150] with him,
But none can drive him from the envious[151] plea   280
Of forfeiture, of justice, and his bond.

JESSICA

When I was with him I have heard him swear

152 *Tubal . . . Chus*; these names come from the Bible (*Genesis*, x.2,6, where the latter appears as *Cush*). They are called *his countrymen* because they are fellow Jews.

153 *It will go hard* – "things will turn out badly".

154 *The best-conditioned . . . courtesies* – "the best natured and most tireless (*unwearied*) spirit in doing generous deeds".

155 *more appears . . . Italy* – "is more evident than in anyone else living (*that draws breath*) in Italy".

156 *deface* – "wipe out, destroy".

it seems to
shylocks planned to come
carry out the way)
all the way)

To Tubal and to Chus,[152] his countrymen,
That he would rather have Antonio's flesh
Than twenty times the value of the sum   285
That he did owe him. And I know, my lord,
If law, authority, and power deny not,
It will go hard[153] with poor Antonio.

PORTIA

Is it your dear friend that is thus in trouble?

BASSANIO

The dearest friend to me, the kindest man,   290
The best-conditioned[154] and unwearied spirit
In doing courtesies, and one in whom
The ancient Roman honour more appears[155]
Than any that draws breath in Italy.

PORTIA

What sum owes he the Jew?   295

BASSANIO

For me, three thousand ducats.

PORTIA

                    What, no more?
Pay him six thousand, and deface[156] the bond;
Double six thousand, and then treble that,
Before a friend of this description
Shall lose a hair through Bassanio's fault.   300
First go with me to church, and call me wife,
And then away to Venice to your friend;
For never shall you lie by Portia's side
With an unquiet soul. You shall have gold
To pay the petty debt twenty times over.   305
When it is paid, bring your true friend along. –
My maid Nerissa and myself meantime

157 *cheer* – "face".

158 *Sweet Bassanio* ... This letter is plainly in accordance with Antonio's character as we have come to know it. His sadness seems to have made it easy for him to resign himself to his fate, and all he asks is to see Bassanio before he dies. Yet such is his love for Bassanio that he will not do anything to persuade him except to appeal to their love for one another.

159 *use your pleasure* – "do as you wish".

160 *Nor rest . . . twain* – "nor shall sleep be a thing which comes between (*'twixt*) us two (*twain*)".

(III.iii) Antonio has now been seized for debt, and walks through the streets of Venice with a gaoler. He has come from prison to plead once more with Shylock, but Shylock refuses to hear him, and Antonio resigns himself to paying his penalty, which falls due the next day. He hopes only that he will be able to see Bassanio before he dies.

Will live as maids and widows. – Come, away!
For you shall hence upon your wedding day.
Bid your friends welcome; show a merry cheer[157] –   310
Since you are dear bought, I will love you dear.
But let me hear the letter of your friend.

BASSANIO [*Reads*].

*Sweet Bassanio,[158] my ships have all miscarried, my creditors grow
cruel, my estate is very low, my bond to the Jew is forfeit, and, since
in paying it it is impossible I should live, all debts are cleared* 315
*between you and I, if I might but see you at my death. Not-
withstanding, use your pleasure;[159] if your love do not persuade
you to come, let not my letter.*

PORTIA

O love, dispatch all business and be gone!

BASSANIO

Since I have your good leave to go away,   320
I will make haste; but, till I come again,
No bed shall e'er be guilty of my stay,
Nor rest[160] be interposer 'twixt us twain.   [*Exeunt*

Scene III. Venice. A street.

Enter SHYLOCK *the Jew, with* SOLANIO, *and* ANTONIO,
and a Gaoler.

SHYLOCK

Gaoler, look to him; tell not me of mercy;
This is the fool that lent out money gratis.
Gaoler, look to him.

ANTONIO

Hear me yet, good Shylock.

1 *naughty* – "wicked".
2 *so fond . . . him* – "so foolish as to come out-of-doors (*abroad*) with him".
3 *dull-eyed* – "easily deceived".
4 *Follow not* – "Don't follow after me". Shylock has turned to walk away and Antonio has begun to follow him, hoping to talk further.
5 *It* – "He".
6 *kept* – "lived".
7 *bootless* – "with no hope of success, useless".

8 *I oft delivered . . . to me* – "I have often freed from bankruptcy actions (*forfeitures*) many people who have from time to time pleaded for help from me (*made moan to me*)". He has often, that is, given money to people whom Shylock has threatened with bankruptcy actions, and thus prevented Shylock from taking legal action against them.
9 *grant . . . hold* – "allow this forfeiture (of a pound of Antonio's flesh) to take effect".

absolute
decision

stubborn.

SHYLOCK

I 'll have my bond; speak not against my bond –
I have sworn an oath that I will have my bond.   5
Thou call'dst me dog before thou hadst a cause,
But since I am a dog, beware my fangs –
The duke shall grant me justice – I do wonder,
Thou naughty[1] gaoler, that thou art so fond[2]
To come abroad with him at his request.   10

ANTONIO

I pray thee hear me speak.

SHYLOCK

I 'll have my bond. I will not hear thee speak;
I 'll have my bond, and therefore speak no more.
I 'll not be made a soft and dull-eyed[3] fool,
To shake the head, relent, and sigh, and yield   15
To Christian intercessors. [*He turns to go*] Follow not[4] –
I 'll have no speaking; I will have my bond.   [*Exit*

SOLANIO

It[5] is the most impenetrable cur
That ever kept[6] with men.

ANTONIO

         Let him alone;
I 'll follow him no more with bootless[7] prayers.   20
He seeks my life, his reason well I know;
I oft delivered[8] from his forfeitures
Many that have at times made moan to me;
Therefore he hates me.

SOLANIO

         I am sure the duke
Will never grant[9] this forfeiture to hold.   25

139

10 *commodity* – "good conditions".
Antonio's argument against an
appeal to the Duke is selfless and
objective: if Shylock is denied his
rights, the reputation which
Venice enjoys for the fair treatment of foreigners would be
greatly damaged (. . . it would
much impeach the justice of the state,
line 29), and this would be most
unfortunate, since the prosperity
of the city depended largely on
foreign trade.

11 *bated* – both "saddened" and
"reduced in weight".

(III.iv) With her husband away, Portia tells Lorenzo and Jessica that she
has made up her mind to retire to a monastery until Bassanio's return. She
asks Lorenzo and Jessica to look after her house for her. But when they have
gone she gives her man a letter to take as quickly as possible to her relative,
Dr. Bellario, who is a lawyer in Padua. She then hints to Nerissa that,
dressed as men, they will soon be seeing their husbands again in Venice.

1 *conceit* – "idea, understanding".
2 *amity* – "friendship". It seems that
they have been talking about the
difference between friendship and
love, and Lorenzo has noticed
how philosophically Portia is
bearing the absence of her husband Bassanio, i.e. how she can
enjoy friendship as well as love.
3 *How true* – "to how true . . ."
4 *lover* – "friend", i.e. Antonio.

5 *Than customary . . . enforce you* –
"than your ordinary acts of kindness would make you".
6 *converse* – "associate".
7 *waste* – "spend".
8 *egall* – "equal".
9 *needs* – "necessarily".
10 *a like proportion . . . spirit* – "a
harmony of characteristics (*lineaments*), habits, and natures".

ANTONIO

The duke cannot deny the course of law;
For the commodity[10] that strangers have
With us in Venice, if it be denied,
Will much impeach the justice of the state,
Since that the trade and profit of the city   30
Consisteth of all nations. Therefore go. –
These griefs and losses have so bated[11] me
That I shall hardly spare a pound of flesh
To-morrow, to my bloody creditor.
Well gaoler, on. – Pray God Bassanio come   35
To see me pay his debt, and then I care not.
                                                    [*Exeunt*

Scene IV. Belmont. A room in Portia's house.

Enter PORTIA, NERISSA, LORENZO, JESSICA, *and*
BALTHAZAR

LORENZO

Madam, although I speak it in your presence,
You have a noble and a true conceit[1]
Of god-like amity,[2] which appears most strongly
In bearing thus the absence of your lord.
But if you knew to whom you show this honour,   5
How true[3] a gentleman you send relief,
How dear a lover[4] of my lord your husband,
I know you would be prouder of the work
Than customary[5] bounty can enforce you.

PORTIA

I never did repent for doing good,   10
Nor shall not now; for in companions
That do converse[6] and waste[7] the time together,
Whose souls do bear an egall[8] yoke of love,
There must be needs[9] a like proportion[10]

11 *bosom lover* – "closest friend".

12 *the semblance of my soul* – "the image of my husband", i.e. Antonio, whom she has reasoned to be very like her husband (*my soul*), because he and Antonio enjoy such a close friendship with one another.

13 *out* – "out of".

14 *husbandry and manage* – "ordering and management".

15 *husband* for *husband's*.

16 *deny this imposition* – "refuse (to carry out) this request".

17 *The which* – "which".

18 *My people*, i.e. Portia's servants. She has already told them what she has decided to do, and they will acknowledge Lorenzo as master of the house and lands.

19 *fare you well* – "may things go well with you; good-bye".

Of lineaments, of manners, and of spirit;   15
Which makes me think that this Antonio,
Being the bosom lover[11] of my lord,
Must needs be like my lord. If it be so,
How little is the cost I have bestowed
In purchasing the semblance of my soul[12]   20
From out[13] the state of hellish cruelty! –
This comes too near the praising of myself;
Therefore no more of it; hear other things. –
Lorenzo, I commit into your hands
The husbandry and manage[14] of my house,   25
Until my lord's return. For mine own part,
I have toward heaven breathed a secret vow
To live in prayer and contemplation,
Only attended by Nerissa here,
Until her husband[15] and my lord's return.   30
There is a monastery two miles off,
And there we will abide. I do desire you
Not to deny this imposition,[16]
The which[17] my love and some necessity
Now lays upon you.

LORENZO

             Madam, with all my heart,   35
I shall obey you in all fair commands.

PORTIA

My people[18] do already know my mind,
And will acknowledge you and Jessica
In place of Lord Bassanio and myself.
So fare you well[19] till we shall meet again.   40

LORENZO

Fair thoughts and happy hours attend on you!

JESSICA

I wish your ladyship all heart's content.

143

20 *Padua* (in Italian *Padova*) is a city in North Italy, not far from Venice. It has an ancient university which was, in the Middle Ages, particularly famous for law studies.

21 *my cousin's hand* – "the hand of my relative".

22 *look* – "see, pay attention to".

23 *imagined speed* – "all imaginable speed".

24 *traject* – "ferry", a place where a boat is regularly available to take people over a short stretch of water.

25 *trades to* – "connects with". The ferry is at a river between Padua and Venice.

26 *convenient* – "due".

27 *habit* – "dress".

28 *accomplished* – "equipped". She means that their husbands will think they are men because they are going to put on men's clothes.

29 *hold . . . wager* – "bet you anything".

30 *accoutered* – "dressed, equipped".

31 *Speak between . . . voice* – "speak as a boy does when his voice is breaking (i.e. when he is changing from a boy into a man), with a voice like a reed pipe".

PORTIA

I thank you for your wish, and am well pleased
To wish it back on you; fare you well, Jessica.

[Exeunt JESSICA *and* LORENZO

Now Balthazar,   45
As I have ever found thee honest-true,
So let me find thee still. Take this same letter,
And use thou all th' endeavour of a man
In speed to Padua.[20] See thou render this
Into my cousin's hand,[21] Doctor Bellario,   50
And look[22] what notes and garments he doth give thee.
Bring them, I pray thee, with imagined speed[23]
Unto the traject,[24] to the common ferry
Which trades to[25] Venice; waste no time in words,
But get thee gone! I shall be there before thee.   55

BALTHAZAR

Madam, I go with all convenient[26] speed.   *[Exit*

PORTIA

Come on, Nerissa, I have work in hand
That you yet know not of; we 'll see our husbands
Before they think of us!

NERISSA

Shall they see us?

PORTIA

They shall, Nerissa, but in such a habit[27]   60
That they shall think we are accomplished[28]
With that we lack. I 'll hold[29] thee any wager,
When we are both accoutered[30] like young men,
I 'll prove the prettier fellow of the two,
And wear my dagger with the braver grace,   65
And speak between[31] the change of man and boy,

145

32 *turn two . . . stride* – "change two of my present ladylike steps into one stride of a man's size".

33 *quaint* – "clever".

34 *Which I denying* – "and when I refused to give it".

35 *I could . . . withal* – "I could not help it".

36 *bragging Jacks* – "boastful fellows".

37 *If thou . . . interpreter* – "if you were near a listener who thought your question indecent".

38 *stays* – "waits".

my coach

(III.v) This scene marks the passing of the time during which Portia and Nerissa carry out their plan to disguise themselves as lawyers. Launcelot talks to Jessica with a great deal of word-play, and the same joking goes on when Lorenzo comes in. But in the end Lorenzo tires of having his words twisted, and when Launcelot leaves he is pleased to talk to Jessica about Portia. Jessica admires her greatly, and speaks too of Bassanio's good fortune in winning her.

1 *look you* – "listen, take notice". They have been talking about Shylock's determination to take revenge.

2 *the sins . . . children*. Launcelot is referring to a passage in the Bible (*Exodus*, xx.5); one of the laws of Moses says that even children and children's children will be punished for the sins of their fathers.

3 *fear* – "fear for".

4 *agitation*; Launcelot probably means to say *cogitation* – "thoughts".

5 *be of good cheer* – "be happy". This phrase may also be a memory from the Bible.

6 *neither* – "indeed".

146

With a reed voice, and turn two[32] mincing steps
Into a manly stride, and speak of frays
Like a fine bragging youth; and tell quaint[33] lies
How honourable ladies sought my love,   70
Which I denying,[34] they fell sick and died.
I could[35] not do withal. Then I 'll repent.
And wish, for all that, that I had not killed them.
And twenty of these puny lies I 'll tell,
That men shall swear I have discontinued school   75
Above a twelvemonth. I have within my mind
A thousand raw tricks of these bragging Jacks[36]
Which I will practise.

NERISSA

Why, shall we turn to men?

PORTIA

Fie! what a question 's that,
If thou[37] wert near a lewd interpreter!   80
But come, I 'll tell thee all my whole device
When I am in my coach, which stays[38] for us
At the park gate; and therefore haste away,
For we must measure twenty miles to-day.   [*Exeunt*

Scene V. Belmont. The garden.

Enter LAUNCELOT *and* JESSICA.

LAUNCELOT

Yes, truly; for look you,[1] the sins[2] of the father are to be
laid upon the children; therefore, I promise you, I fear[3] you. I
was always plain with you, and so now I speak my agitation[4]
of the matter; therefore be of good cheer,[5] for truly I think
you are damned. There is but one hope in it that can do you   5
any good, and that is but a kind of bastard hope neither.[6]

147

7 *sins ... upon me.* This is an echo of the first lines of the scene. But here, in the circumstances described, she would be punished for the sins of her mother, not her father.

8 *Scylla ... Charybdis.* In an old Greek story, a nymph called Scylla was turned into a monster, and lived as such in a cave by the Straits of Messina between Sicily and the Italian mainland. She tried to catch seamen who had to pass between her cave and the whirlpool of Charybdis. (The story is in Homer's *Odyssey*, xii.235 ff.) The phrase "between Scylla and Charybdis" came to be used for situations where two alternative conditions were both dangerous.

9 *he hath ... Christian.* It is suggested in the Bible (1 *Corinthians*, vii.14) that if one partner in a marriage is Christian, the other is "sanctified", i.e. made holy.

10 *the more to blame he* – "he is the more blameworthy".

11 *we were ... before* – "there were enough (*enow*) of us Christians already".

12 *e'en* for *even*.

13 *one by another* – "together".

14 *pork-eaters*: unlike Jews, who will not eat pork.

15 *a rasher on the coals.* This phrase is certainly connected with *pork* in the previous line, (*rasher* – "slice of bacon"), but its meaning is not very clear. Perhaps a rasher cooked on the coals was a poor man's meal.

16 *corners* – "out-of-the-way places". They are somewhere in the garden of Belmont.

JESSICA

And what hope is that, I pray thee?

LAUNCELOT

Marry, you may partly hope that your father got you not, that you are not the Jew's daughter.

JESSICA

That were a kind of bastard hope indeed; – so the sins[7] of my mother should be visited upon me.

LAUNCELOT

Truly, then I fear you are damned both by father and mother; thus when I shun Scylla,[8] your father, I fall into Charybdis, your mother; well, you are gone both ways.

JESSICA

I shall be saved by my husband; he hath[9] made me a Christian!

LAUNCELOT

Truly, the more to blame he;[10] we were[11] Christians enow before, e'en[12] as many as could well live one by another.[13] This making of Christians will raise the price of hogs – if we grow all to be pork-eaters,[14] we shall not shortly have a rasher on the coals[15] for money.

Enter LORENZO

JESSICA

I'll tell my husband, Launcelot, what you say; here he comes!

LORENZO

I shall grow jealous of you shortly, Launcelot, if you thus get my wife into corners![16]

17 *are out* – "have quarrelled".

18 *commonwealth* – "state".

19 *I shall answer ... Launcelot!* (line 31). This passage has not been satisfactorily explained. In the first part, Lorenzo means that, far from being a bad member of the state, he will be a good member, since (he implies) he will have children who will profit the commonwealth. The rest may refer to some incident which Shakespeare's audience knew about but which cannot now be traced; or maybe *the Moor*, a black woman, is one in the train of the Prince of Morocco. In any case, calling her *the Moor* gives Launcelot an opportunity to play on *Moor* and *more* in his next speech.

20 *more than reason* – "larger than what is reasonable".

21 *best grace of wit* – "the wittiest and most elegant conversation". Lorenzo is saying in effect that if *wit* is reduced to the level of Launcelot's childish word-play, conversation will be nothing but parrot-like repetition. It is appropriate that Lorenzo should notice this, because he himself obviously enjoys elegant styles of conversation, e.g. in his lines at II.vi.53–7.

22 *stomachs* – "appetites"; so they are, in fact, "prepared" for dinner.

23 *Goodly* – "Gracious".

24 *cover* – "lay the table", i.e. the dinner is ready and they need only lay the table. But, having made Lorenzo use the word *cover*, Launcelot deliberately misunderstands him, and takes it in the other sense common in Shakespeare's day, "put one's hat on". He will not do this in the presence of Lorenzo and Jessica, saying (line 44), *I know my duty*.

JESSICA

Nay, you need not fear us, Lorenzo; Launcelot and I are
out.[17] He tells me flatly there 's no mercy for me in heaven, 25
because I am a Jew's daughter; and he says you are no
good member of the commonwealth,[18] for in converting
Jews to Christians you raise the price of pork.

LORENZO

I shall answer[19] that better to the commonwealth than you
can the getting up of the negro's belly; the Moor is with 30
child by you, Launcelot!

LAUNCELOT

It is much that the Moor should be more than reason;[20] but
if she be less than an honest woman, she is indeed more than
I took her for.

LORENZO

How every fool can play upon the word! I think the best 35
grace of wit[21] will shortly turn into silence, and discourse
grow commendable in none only but parrots. – Go in, sirrah;
bid them prepare for dinner!

LAUNCELOT

That is done, sir; they have all stomachs![22]

LORENZO

Goodly[23] Lord, what a wit-snapper are you! then bid them 40
prepare dinner!

LAUNCELOT

That is done too, sir, only "cover" [24] is the word.

LORENZO

Will you cover then, sir?

LAUNCELOT

Not so, sir, neither; I know my duty.

25 *quarrelling with occasion* – "disagreeing in words on every possible occasion".

26 *For* – "As for".

27 *table* – "food for the meal". He has changed the orders by changing the arrangement and meaning of the words. So *covered* in the following line he changes to mean "served in a covered dish".

28 *as humours . . . govern* – "as your inclinations and personal opinions shall order".

29 *O dear discretion* – "O affected, unnatural distinctions between words".

30 *suited* – "made to suit the occasion (literally)".

31 *fool* – "clown".

32 *A many* – "many".

33 *stand . . . place* – "have a better position", as clowns in courts.

34 *Garnished like him*: this may mean, (1) "fitted out (with the dress of a court clown) like he is"; or, (2) "equipped like him (with an *army of good words*, line 55)". If (2) is the correct one, then Lorenzo must be praising Launcelot for learning all these tricks with words, for they may at least get him a better position, as they have done other fools.

35 *for a . . . matter* – "who ignore the sense of a conversation (*matter*) in order to bring in amusing word-play".

36 *How cheer'st thou* – "How are you".

37 *meet* – "appropriate".

38 *merit it.* The earliest editions of the play have *meane it* in place of *merit* in the text here. It is difficult to see the sense of "mean" in this passage, and the change to *merit* (first suggested by the poet Alexander Pope) gives good sense: if Bassanio did not deserve, through his uprightness, the almost heavenly joys of having Portia as his wife, this would have been enough reward for him, and he would not merit the heavenly joys of the next world.

39 *Pawned* – "wagered"; something else would have to be wagered with the other woman, for she could not by herself equal Portia.

40 *rude* – "simple".

LORENZO

Yet more quarrelling with occasion![25] Wilt thou show the   45
whole wealth of thy wit in an instant? I pray thee understand
a plain man in his plain meaning: go to thy fellows, bid them
cover the table, serve in the meat, and we will come in to
dinner.

LAUNCELOT

For[26] the table,[27] sir, it shall be served in; for the meat, sir,   50
it shall be covered. For your coming in to dinner, sir, why, let
it be as humours[28] and conceits shall govern.   [*Exit*

LORENZO

O dear discretion,[29] how his words are suited![30]
The fool[31] hath planted in his memory
An army of good words, and I do know   55
A many[32] fools that stand[33] in better place,
Garnished like him,[34] that for a[35] tricksy word
Defy the matter. How cheer'st thou,[36] Jessica?
And now, good sweet, say thy opinion,
How dost thou like the Lord Bassanio's wife?   60

JESSICA

Past all expressing; it is very meet[37]
The Lord Bassanio live an upright life
For, having such a blessing in his lady,
He finds the joys of heaven here on earth,
And if on earth he do not merit it,[38]   65
In reason he should never come to heaven!
Why, if two gods should play some heavenly match,
And on the wager lay two earthly women,
And Portia one, there must·be something else
Pawned[39] with the other, for the poor rude[40] world   70
Hath not her fellow.

41 *stomach* – (1) "inclination (to praise)", and (2) "appetite (for food)".

42 *howsome'er* – "in whatever way".

43 *'mong* for *among*.

44 *I'll set you forth* – (1) "praise you at length", and (2) "set the meal in front of you".

LORENZO

          Even such a husband
Hast thou of me, as she is for a wife.

JESSICA

Nay, but ask my opinion too of that.

LORENZO

I will anon; first, let us go to dinner.

JESSICA

Nay, let me praise you while I have a stomach.[41]   75

LORENZO

No, pray thee, let it serve for table-talk;
Then, howsome'er[42] thou speak'st, 'mong[43] other things
I shall digest it.

JESSICA

       Well, I'll set you forth.[44]

                       [*Exeunt*

ACT FOUR

(IV.i) The court scene begins with the Duke, and Antonio and his friends, talking together about Shylock and the demands of the bond. When Shylock enters, the Duke questions him on his cruel desires, but the talk proves useless because Shylock is determined to make Antonio suffer. The Duke will not decide the case, but tells how he has asked Bellario, a judge from Padua, to come to the court. Nerissa then enters, dressed as a lawyer's clerk, and brings a letter from Bellario, as already arranged by Portia. Shylock is by now sharpening his knife in readiness for cutting Antonio's flesh. The letter is read; in it Bellario says he is ill and is sending a young lawyer, Balthazar, in his place. "Balthazar" comes in; it is Portia, dressed as a doctor of laws, but no one recognizes her. She assumes the position of judge and begins to talk to Shylock of mercy. Shylock refuses to show any mercy, and Antonio says that he is quite resigned to his fate.

But suddenly things take a different turn. Portia says that no blood may be spilt when the flesh is cut off, and if the flesh is the slightest amount more or less than one pound, Shylock will lose all his property. These conditions are impossible to fulfil, and it is Shylock's turn to ask for help; he says he will accept the offer already made of three times the amount of the loan, but Portia will not allow it. Then he is told of another law which punishes anyone who seeks the life of another; under this law, half the offender's property goes to the Duke and half to the person wronged. The court is merciful, and it is decided that the state fines him, that he must become a Christian, and that at his death all his property must go to his son-in-law and daughter, Lorenzo and Jessica.

When Shylock goes out, Portia says she is ready to leave at once for Padua. Bassanio tries to persuade the "judge" to accept a reward, but Portia at first refuses. But since Bassanio presses further, Portia asks for his gloves and the ring on his finger. He at first refuses to give the ring, saying it was given him by his wife. At this Portia leaves. But Antonio persuades him to change his mind, and Bassanio sends the ring after her.

The climax of this moving scene is when Portia begins to turn the case against Shylock. His evil purposes and Antonio's melancholy make much of the scene tragic, but the sadness is lightened by the humour of the disguise; Bassanio, pleading in fiery words for his friend, does not know that he is talking to his wife, so that when the "judge" asks for his ring, and gets it, Portia makes him break his promise to her never to sell it, lose it, or give it away. This leads into a similar trick which Nerissa intends to play on Gratiano, as explained in the next scene.

1 *Magnificoes* – "chief men" (of Venice). The word was used before at III.ii.278.
2 *What* is used by the Duke to get people's attention.

3 *Ready* – "Here".
4 *From any ... mercy.* – "of the smallest amount of mercy".
5 *qualify* – "make more moderate".
6 *that* – "because".

continued on page 160

158

ACT FOUR

Scene I. Venice. A Court of Justice.

Enter the DUKE, *the Magnificoes,*[1] ANTONIO, BASSANIO, *and* GRATIANO, SALERIO *and others.*

DUKE

What,[2] is Antonio here?

ANTONIO

Ready,[3] so please your grace!

DUKE

I am sorry for thee; thou art come to answer
A stony adversary, an inhuman wretch,
Uncapable of pity, void and empty
From any[4] dram of mercy.

*Not
disinterested
Jew. (inpartial
* though you
should be*

ANTONIO

I have heard
Your grace hath ta'en great pains to qualify[5]
His rigorous course; but since he stands obdurate,
And that[6] no lawful means can carry me
Out of his envy's reach,[7] I do oppose[8]   10
My patience to his fury, and am armed
To suffer with a quietness of spirit
The very tyranny[9] and rage of his.

*emphasises
christian virtues
(patience/
endurance)*

DUKE

Go, one,[10] call the Jew into the court.

SALERIO

He is ready at the door; he comes, my lord.   15

Enter SHYLOCK.

159

7 *his envy's reach* – "the reach of his desire to hurt others".

8 *do oppose . . . fury* – "set up my patience in opposition to his fury".

9 *tyranny* – "violence".

10 *one* – "someone".

11 *our* for *my*, a form often used by kings and other governors when speaking of themselves; so *we*, when used by these speakers, can mean "I".

12 *this fashion . . . malice* – "this outward show of your ill-will".

13 *remorse* – "pity".

14 *where* – "in contrast with the fact that".

15 *loose* – "go without".

16 *moiety of the principal* – "part of the money actually lent", the interest on which is to be paid for the loan.

17 *royal merchant* – "merchant prince", a merchant of great wealth and high social position.

18 *pluck . . . flint* – "snatch feelings of pity for his condition (*state*) from breasts of brass (i.e. those that are not soft to appeals) and hard hearts of stone".

19 *Turks . . . Tartars* signify only people from the East who were not Christians.

20 *offices* – "practices, moral duties".

21 *gentle* – perhaps playing on *Gentile*. Shylock's splendid speech which follows gives a sort of reason for the action he hopes to carry out against Antonio: there are people who have an uncontrollable dislike for a certain thing, and it is small matters like these dislikes which determine their actions. He hates Antonio, he says, and that is sufficient explanation for what he intends to do.

22 *possessed . . . of* – "told".

23 *the danger light Upon* – "the harm come to"; *light* here is a form of *alight* – "come down".

24 *Three thousand ducats.* With Portia's help, Antonio is now certainly able to meet his debts; but for Shylock the period of the bond has gone by and he will make Antonio pay the penalty instead.

25 *humour* – "passing fancy"; but he may at the same time wish *humour* to refer to his character in general, a course which would confuse still further his reasons for insisting on the forfeiture.

26 *baned* – "poisoned".

27 *a gaping pig*: this must refer to the roasted head of a pig which was sometimes served in Shakespeare's day as food for the table.

humiliation to shylock by Authority

DUKE

Make room, and let him stand before our[11] face.
Shylock, the world thinks, and I think so too,
That thou but leadest this fashion[12] of thy malice
To the last hour of act, and then 't is thought
Thou 'lt show thy mercy and remorse,[13] more strange
Than is thy strange apparent cruelty;
And where[14] thou now exact'st the penalty,
Which is a pound of this poor merchant's flesh,
Thou wilt not only loose[15] the forfeiture,
But, touched with human gentleness and love,
Forgive a moiety of the principal,[16]
Glancing an eye of pity on his losses
That have of late so huddled on his back
Enow to press a royal merchant[17] down,
And pluck[18] commiseration of his state
From brassy bosoms and rough hearts of flint,
From stubborn Turks,[19] and Tartars never trained
To offices[20] of tender courtesy.
We all expect a gentle[21] answer, Jew!

learning, Against shylock. one sided

.20

forgiveness is informed in New Test.

30

— Duke expects 'gentileness'.

SHYLOCK

I have possessed[22] your grace of what I purpose,   35
And by our holy Sabbath have I sworn
To have the due and forfeit of my bond.
If you deny it, let the danger light
Upon[23] your charter and your city's freedom!
You 'll ask me why I rather choose to have   40
A weight of carrion flesh than to receive
Three thousand ducats.[24] I' ll not answer that!
But say it is my humour[25] – is it answered?
What if my house be troubled with a rat,
And I be pleased to give ten thousand ducats   45
To have it baned?[26] – what, are you answered yet?
Some men there are love not a gaping pig;[27]

saying it would deny the law.

Justifying cruelty.

28 *the bagpipe . . . nose*: bagpipes are pipes for playing music which are fixed into a bag – in this case Shylock is thinking of a bag wrapped in woollen cloth (see line 56 below). The noise they made sounded to some like humming through the nose.

29 *affection . . . loathes* (line 52). The earliest editions have a different punctuation from that given here, but do not seem to make good sense. It is fairly certain that *affection* and *passion* are to be contrasted, as at III.i.48. The meaning then is: "one's inclination (*affection*), the master of deeper feeling (*passion*), controls it (the deeper feeling) in accordance with what it likes and dislikes".

30 *he*, i.e. one person . . . *he*, another, and so on.

31 *of force* – "of necessity".

32 *himself being offended* – "when he himself is offended (by something he dislikes, such as a gaping pig, a cat or a bagpipe)"; he then cannot help offending others, e.g. by becoming very angry.

33 *lodged* – "firmly fixed".

34 *certain* – "determined".

35 *losing*, since Shylock will lose his money if the case goes in his favour, and will get only a *weight of carrion flesh* (line 41 above) instead.

Some that are mad if they behold a cat;
And others, when the bagpipe[28] sings i' the' nose,
Cannot contain their urine – for affection,[29]   50
Master of passion, sways it to the mood
Of what it likes or loathes. Now for your answer:
As there is no firm reason to be rendered
Why *he*[30] cannot abide a gaping pig,
Why *he* a harmless, necessary cat,   55
Why *he* a woollen bagpipe, but of force[31]
Must yield to such inevitable shame
As to offend, himself being offended;[32]
So can I give no reason, nor I will not,
More than a lodged[33] hate and a certain[34] loathing   60
·I bear Antonio, that I follow thus
A losing[35] suit against him! – Are you answered?

} purposely
ridiculous
example.

BASSANIO

This is no answer, thou unfeeling man,
To excuse the current of thy cruelty.

SHYLOCK

I am not bound to please thee with my answers!   65

BASSANIO

Do all men kill the things they do not love?

SHYLOCK

Hates any man the thing he would not kill?

BASSANIO

Every offence is not a hate at first!

SHYLOCK

What! wouldst thou have a serpent sting thee twice?

163

36 *think you ... Jew* – "remember that you are disputing with a Jew".

37 *the main flood bate* – "the high tide bring down".

38 *fretten*, a less usual form of *fretted* – "disturbed, ruffled".

39 *all brief ... conveniency* – "all convenient speed and plainness".

40 *draw* – "take".

41 *rendering none* – "since you show none".

42 *parts* – "duties".

43 *burthens*, an old form of *burdens*.

Handwritten annotations: dignity concerns for noble death by turning the other cheek. Antonio says: Jew's hatred is elemental force untouched by reason

ANTONIO

I pray you think you³⁶ question with the Jew.
You may as well go stand upon the beach
And bid the main flood bate³⁷ his usual height;
You may as well use question with the wolf,
Why he hath made the ewe bleat for the lamb;
You may as well forbid the mountain pines
To wag their high tops, and to make no noise
When they are fretten³⁸ with the gusts of heaven;
You may as well do anything most hard
As seek to soften that – than which what's harder? –
His Jewish heart! Therefore, I do beseech you,   80
Make no more offers, use no farther means,
But with all brief³⁹ and plain conveniency
Let me have judgement, and the Jew his will!

BASSANIO

For thy three thousand ducats, here is six!

SHYLOCK

If every ducat in six thousand ducats   85
Were in six parts, and every part a ducat,
I would not draw⁴⁰ them; I would have my bond!

DUKE

How shalt thou hope for mercy, rendering none?⁴¹

SHYLOCK

What judgement shall I dread, doing no wrong?
You have among you many a purchased slave,   90
Which, like your asses, and your dogs and mules,
You use in abject and in slavish parts,⁴²
Because you bought them; shall I say to you,
Let them be free, marry them to your heirs?
Why sweat they under burthens?⁴³ let their beds   95

44 *palates Be seasoned* – "tastes be attracted".
45 *viands* – "foods".
46 *fie upon* – "a curse on".
47 *Upon my power* – "In accordance with my authority".
48 *doctor,* i.e. doctor of laws.
49 *here stays without* – "there waits outside".

50 *a tainted ... flock* – "a diseased, unfruitful ram of the flock". He has already used the imagery of the flock (lines 73–4) in another connection; now he refers it directly to himself. His sadness has been made deeper by his losses and he feels himself to be more than ever apart from society. This thought leads him to the depths; in the following line he is not far from suggesting that he becomes a sacrifice to friendship (*Meetest* – "most suitable" – *for death*). (See Introduction, p. xxiii.)

Be made as soft as yours, and let their palates
Be seasoned[44] with such viands?[45] You will answer
"The slaves are ours." – So do I answer you:
The pound of flesh which I demand of him
Is dearly bought, 't is mine and I will have it;
If you deny me, fie upon[46] your law!
There is no force in the decrees of Venice!
I stand for judgement; answer, shall I have it?

100

DUKE

Upon my power[47] I may dismiss this court,
Unless Bellario, a learned doctor,[48]
Whom I have sent for to determine this,
Come here to-day.

105

SALERIO

My lord, here stays without[49]
A messenger with letters from the doctor,
New come from Padua.

DUKE

Bring us the letters! call the messenger!

110

BASSANIO

Good cheer, Antonio! what, man, courage yet!
The Jew shall have my flesh, blood, bones and all,
Ere thou shalt lose for me one drop of blood.

ANTONIO

I am a tainted[50] wether of the flock,
Meetest for death; the weakest kind of fruit
Drops earliest to the ground, and so let me;
You cannot better be employed, Bassanio,
Than to live still and write mine epitaph.

115

Enter NERISSA, *dressed like a lawyer's clerk.*

167

51 *sole* and *soul* are now pronounced the same; in Shakespeare's day, if not the same, they were pronounced very much alike.

52 *hangman* – "executioner".

53 *pierce thee*, i.e. "pierce your ears", "affect you".

54 *inexorable* – "unyielding" (the normal modern sense); the earliest editions of the play have *inexecrable,* which is unknown elsewhere and is probably an error for *inexorable.*

55 *for thy life . . . accused* – "let justice itself be accused for allowing you to live"; i.e. if Shylock is allowed to live, then there must be some fault with Justice.

56 *Pythagoras,* an ancient Greek philosopher, believed that at death the souls of men and animals moved to other bodies. Gratiano, a Christian, does not believe in this theory, but the sight of Shylock almost makes him *waver* (line 130) – "hesitate" – in his faith and see Shylock as an example of Pythagoras' belief: when Shylock was still unborn, he imagines, the spirit of a murderous wolf moved into his body.

57 *trunks* – "bodies".

58 *his fell soul fleet* – "his cruel spirit fly away".

59 *dam* – "mother", particularly the mother of an animal or monster.

DUKE

Came you from Padua, from Bellario?

NERISSA

From both, my lord. Bellario greets your grace.   120

[She gives him a letter

BASSANIO

Why dost thou whet thy knife so earnestly?

SHYLOCK

To cut the forfeiture from that bankrupt there!

GRATIANO

Not on thy sole,[51] but on thy soul, harsh Jew,
Thou mak'st thy knife keen; but no metal can,
No, not the hangman's[52] axe, bear half the keenness   125
Of thy sharp envy. Can no prayers pierce thee?[53]

SHYLOCK

No, none that *thou* hast wit enough to make.

GRATIANO

O, be thou damned, inexorable[54] dog!
And for thy life[55] let justice be accused;
Thou almost mak'st me waver in my faith   130
To hold opinion with Pythagoras,[56]
That souls of animals infuse themselves
Into the trunks[57] of men: thy currish spirit
Governed a wolf, who, hanged for human slaughter,
Even from the gallows did his fell soul fleet,[58]   135
And, whilst thou layest in thy unhallowed dam,[59]
Infused itself in thee; for thy desires
Are wolvish, bloody, starved, and ravenous.

Shylock's
unmorality

169

60 *Thou but offend'st* – "you only injure".
61 *cureless* – "incurable, without remedy".
62 *hard by* – "near by".
63 *in loving visitation* – "on a friendly visit".
64 *stead* – "place".
65 *his lack of years* – "his youth".
66 *whose trial . . . commendation* – "for his trial (i.e. your trial of him in my place) will make this recommendation of him more obvious".

the seal from off my bond

SHYLOCK

Till thou canst rail the seal from off my bond,
Thou but offend'st[60] thy lungs to speak so loud;   140
Repair thy wit, good youth, or it will fall
To cureless[61] ruin. I stand here for law.

DUKE

This letter from Bellario doth commend
A young and learned doctor to our court.
Where is he?

NERISSA

                He attendeth here hard by[62]   145
To know your answer, whether you 'll admit him.

DUKE

With all my heart; some three or four of you
Go give him courteous conduct to this place;
Meantime the court shall hear Bellario's letter.

[Reads] *Your grace shall understand that at the receipt of your* 150
letter I am very sick, but in the instant that your messenger came, in
loving visitation[63] *was with me a young doctor of Rome; his name*
is Balthazar. I acquainted him with the cause in controversy between
the Jew and Antonio the merchant; we turned o'er many books
together; he is furnished with my opinion, which, bettered with his 155
own learning, the greatness whereof I cannot enough commend,
comes with him at my importunity, to fill up your grace's request
in my stead.[64] *I beseech you let his lack of years*[65] *be no impediment*
to let him lack a reverend estimation, for I never knew so young a
body with so old a head. I leave him to your gracious acceptance, 160
whose trial[66] *shall better publish his commendation.*

Enter PORTIA, *dressed as* BALTHAZAR, *a doctor of laws.*

You hear the learn'd Bellario what he writes,
[*He sees* PORTIA] And here, I take it, is the doctor come.
[*To* PORTIA] Give me your hand. Came you from old
    Bellario?   165

171

67 *difference* – "dispute".
68 *holds this present question* – "causes this present enquiry to be held".
69 *throughly* for *thoroughly*.
70 *Yet in such rule* – "yet it is in such good order".

71 *Then must . . . merciful* – "Then the Jew will, of course, be merciful"; Portia tries to persuade him by implying that there is no doubt about the matter. But Shylock misunderstands her, taking *must* to mean that he is compelled to be so. He then wants to know whose authority will compel him.

dressed as BALTHAZAR, *a doctor of laws*

172

PORTIA

I did, my lord.

DUKE

You are welcome; take your place;
Are you acquainted with the difference[67]
That holds this present question[68] in the court?

PORTIA

I am informéd throughly[69] of the cause.
Which is the merchant here? and which the Jew?

DUKE

Antonio and old Shylock, both stand forth.

PORTIA

Is your name Shylock?

SHYLOCK

Shylock is my name.

PORTIA

Of a strange nature is the suit you follow,
Yet in such rule[70] that the Venetian law
Cannot impugn you as you do proceed.   175
[*To* ANTONIO] You stand within his danger, do you not?

ANTONIO

Ay, so he says.

PORTIA

Do you confess the bond?

ANTONIO

I do.

PORTIA

Then must[71] the Jew be merciful.

*Closeness
in the   170
two, as
well as
portia's
disguise*

173

72 *strained* – "constrained, forced", i.e. mercy is not a matter of compulsion, as Shylock has implied, but comes freely.

73 *twice blest* – "doubly full of blessing".

74 *'Tis mightiest ... mightiest* – "It (mercy) is most powerful in those who use their power best"; this is probably the best explanation, though some have thought that *the mightiest* may refer to God, the Almighty.

75 *His sceptre.* The sceptre of a king is a rod, usually made of some precious metal, which symbolizes his authority, *the force of* his *temporal* ("earthly") *power.*

76 *this sceptred sway* – "rule symbolized by this sceptre".

77 *earthly power ... justice* – "when justice is moderated with mercy, earthly power looks most like the power of God".

78 *in the course ... salvation* – "if justice took its course (without mercy), none of our souls would be saved". If we are to be blessed in heaven, we shall depend upon the mercy of God, not only on justice; for we are all sinful, and deserve punishment.

79 *that same prayer ...* This is an echo of the Lord's prayer from the Bible: "And forgive us our debts, as we forgive our debtors" (*Matthew* vi.12), or the Prayer Book version: "And forgive us our trespasses, As we forgive them that trespass against us." Portia is using a Christian argument to persuade the Jew to show mercy.

80 *mitigate* – "moderate (with mercy)".

81 *My deeds upon my head* – "I take the responsibility for what I do"; the talk about salvation has not persuaded him, and he wants justice.

82 *here I tender it ...* It is Bassanio, not Antonio, who answers readily to the question about payment. As before (lines 112–3 above), Bassanio is very ready to offer his life to save his friend; he offers his hands, head, and heart, not just a pound of flesh, for forfeiture against the payment of ten times the loan (line 208).

Mercy is a feminine quality ∴ Portia says this.

174

SHYLOCK

On what compulsion must I? tell me that.

PORTIA

The quality of mercy is not strained;[72]   180
It droppeth as the gentle rain from heaven
Upon the place beneath; it is twice blest:[73]
It blesseth him that gives, and him that takes;
'T is mightiest[74] in the mightiest; it becomes
The thronéd monarch better than his crown.   185
His sceptre[75] shows the force of temporal power,
The attribute to awe and majesty,
Wherein doth sit the dread and fear of kings;
But mercy is above this sceptred sway;[76]
It is enthronéd in the hearts of kings;   190
It is an attribute to God himself;
And earthly power[77] doth then show likest God's
When mercy seasons justice. Therefore, Jew,
Though justice be thy plea, consider this,
That in the course[78] of justice none of us   195
Should see salvation; we do pray for mercy,
And that same prayer[79] doth teach us all to render
The deeds of mercy. I have spoke thus much
To mitigate[80] the justice of thy plea,
Which, if thou follow, this strict court of Venice   200
Must needs give sentence 'gainst the merchant there.

SHYLOCK

My deeds upon my head![81] I crave the law,
The penalty and forfeit of my bond.

PORTIA

Is he not able to discharge the money?

BASSANIO

Yes, here I tender it[82] for him in the court;   205

83 *malice bears down truth* – "malice (on Shylock's part) has overcome honesty (the rightness of paying back twice the amount of the loan)".

84 *Wrest once ... authority* – "on this one occasion (*once*) make the law bend to your authority".

85 *for* – "as".

86 *error* – "wrong judgement".

87 *Daniel* was a young man who acted as a judge in the story of Susanna and the Elders in the Bible. Susanna is falsely accused by the Elders of Israel, and is saved by Daniel, a wise young man, who turns the words of the Elders in such a way that they accuse themselves. So Portia appears as a young man and later (lines 321 ff.) turns the words of the bond in such a way that the accuser, Shylock, cannot act further; then it is Gratiano who calls her a Daniel (line 329). The name Daniel means, in Hebrew, "God is my iudge".

Orb and sceptre [75]

Yea, twice the sum; if that will not suffice,
I will be bound to pay it ten times o'er
On forfeit of my hands, my head, my heart;
If this will not suffice, it must appear
That malice bears down truth.[83] And I beseech you   210
Wrest once[84] the law to your authority;
To do a great right, do a little wrong,
And curb this cruel devil of his will.

asking to bend the law.

PORTIA

It must not be; there is no power in Venice
Can alter a decree establishéd;
'T will be recorded for[85] a precedent,   215
And many an error[86] by the same example
Will rush into the state. It cannot be.

Law is crucial to a successful society.

SHYLOCK

A Daniel[87] come to judgement! yea, a Daniel!
O wise young judge, how I do honour thee!   220

PORTIA

I pray you let me look upon the bond.

SHYLOCK

Here 't is, most reverend doctor, here it is.

PORTIA

Shylock, there 's thrice thy money offered thee.

SHYLOCK

An oath, an oath, I have an oath in heaven. –
Shall I lay perjury upon my soul?   225
No, not for Venice.

PORTIA

        Why, this bond is forfeit,
And lawfully by this the Jew may claim

88 *tear* – "tear up, destroy".
89 *tenor* – "true purpose (of the bond)".
90 *charge* – "bid".
91 *pillar* – "main support".
92 *I stay here on* – "I keep to dependence upon".

93 *Hath full relation to* – "fully allows and enforces", i.e. the penalty demanded is in full accordance with the law. Shylock is delighted to know this, and praises "the judge" even more highly.
94 *more elder* – "older".

A pound of flesh, to be by him cut off
Nearest the merchant's heart. [*To* SHYLOCK] Be merciful,
Take thrice thy money; bid me tear[88] the bond.   230

SHYLOCK

When it is paid, according to the tenor.[89]
It doth appear you are a worthy judge,
You know the law; your exposition
Hath been most sound. I charge[90] you by the law,
Whereof you are a well-deserving pillar,[91]   235
Proceed to judgement; by my soul I swear,
There is no power in the tongue of man
To alter me. I stay here on[92] my bond.

ANTONIO

Most heartily I do beseech the court
To give the judgement.

PORTIA

        Why then thus it is: 240
You must prepare your bosom for his knife.

SHYLOCK

O noble judge! O excellent young man!

PORTIA

For the intent and purpose of the law
Hath full relation to[93] the penalty,
Which here appeareth due upon the bond.   245

SHYLOCK

'T is very true. O wise and upright judge,
How much more elder[94] art thou than thy looks!

PORTIA

[*To* ANTONIO] Therefore, lay bare your bosom.

95 *balance* – "scales".
96 *on your charge* – "to be paid for by you".

97 *nominated* – "stated".
98 *still her use* – "always her (Fortune's) custom".

SHYLOCK

                Ay, his breast,
So says the bond, doth it not, noble judge?
"Nearest his heart", those are the very words.   250

PORTIA

It is so. Are there balance[95] here to weigh
The flesh?

SHYLOCK

      I have them ready.

PORTIA

Have by some surgeon, Shylock, on your charge,[96]
To stop his wounds, lest he do bleed to death.

SHYLOCK

Is it so nominated[97] in the bond?   255

PORTIA

It is not so expressed, but what of that?
'T were good you do so much for charity.

SHYLOCK

I cannot find it; 't is not in the bond.

PORTIA

[*To* ANTONIO] You merchant, have you anything to say?

ANTONIO

But little. I am armed and well prepared.   260
Give me your hand, Bassanio; fare you well,
Grieve not that I am fall'n to this for you,
For herein Fortune shows herself more kind
Than is her custom. It is still her use[98]

99 *hollow eye . . . wrinkled brow.* These are the signs of worry and unhappiness in a man. Antonio has noticed that *Fortune* ("Fate") has a way of letting a rich man live on after all his riches have gone. Fortune is, he thinks, soon to take him away, by death, from such unhappiness (*cut me off*, line 268).

100 *the process . . . end* – "what took place at Antonio's death".

101 *speak me . . . death* – "speak well of me at the time of my death".

102 *a love* – "a friend who loved him dearly".

103 *Repent but you that* – "Only repent that". All Antonio seems to want from Bassanio is some feeling of sadness that their close friendship is now at an end.

104 *with all my heart.* Antonio plays on the two meanings of this phrase: (1) "with the greatest pleasure", and (2) literally, "with the whole of my heart", which will unavoidably come out when the Jew takes a pound of flesh from his breast. It is a sign of Antonio's resignation and melancholy that he can joke when death seems so near.

105 *I would lose all . . .* Bassanio has already been free with such promises, and no one seems to take him very seriously; see lines 112–13 above. Here Portia, in the following two lines, brings Bassanio back to earth again by mentioning his wife, who is, of course, "the judge", though Bassanio does not know it. These lines of Portia are fittingly in a very conversational style, in contrast to the formal speech of Bassanio which has gone before. The lines are thus a delightful example of Portia's humour.

106 *protest* – "declare".

107 *I would . . . heaven, so . . .* – "I could wish she were in heaven (i.e. dead), provided that . . ." By saying this Gratiano only makes matters worse, and Nerissa, like Portia, gives a very down-to-earth comment.

108 *else* – "otherwise"

To let the wretched man outlive his wealth, 265
To view with hollow eye[99] and wrinkled brow
An age of poverty: from which ling'ring penance
Of such misery doth she cut me off.
Commend me to your honourable wife;
Tell her the process[100] of Antonio's end, 270
Say how I loved you, speak me[101] fair in death;
And when the tale is told, bid her be judge
Whether Bassanio had not once a love;[102]
Repent but you that[103] you shall lose your friend
And he repents not that he pays your debt. 275
For if the Jew do cut but deep enough,
I'll pay it instantly, with all my heart.[104]

BASSANIO

Antonio, I am married to a wife
Which is as dear to me as life itself,
But life itself, my wife, and all the world, 280
Are not with me esteemed above thy life.
I would lose all,[105] ay, sacrifice them all
Here to this devil, to deliver you.

PORTIA

Your wife would give you little thanks for that
If she were by to hear you make the offer. 285

GRATIANO

I have a wife who I protest[106] I love –
I would[107] she were in heaven, so she could
Entreat some power to change this currish Jew.

NERISSA

'T is well you offer it behind her back;
The wish would make else[108] an unquiet house. 290

109 *Would any . . . husband* – "I wish she had married *any* descendant of Barabbas (i.e. any Jew, however bad)". Barabbas was a Jewish thief and revolutionary who was set free at the time Jesus was killed (*Mark*, xv.6–15). The rhythm of the line makes it necessary to accent Bárabbás, on the first and last syllables, not the middle one as it is pronounced today.

110 *trifle* – "waste".

111 *Tarry* – "Wait".

112 *Mark* – "Notice". Bassanio wants Shylock to notice not only the new turn which events have taken but also that he is using Shylock's own words, *upright* (line 246), *learned* (line 300).

SHYLOCK

[*Aside*] These be the Christian husbands! I have a daughter –
Would any[109] of the stock of Barabbas
Had been her husband, rather than a Christian.
[*Aloud*] We trifle[110] time; I pray thee pursue sentence.

PORTIA

A pound of that same merchant's flesh is thine;   295
The court awards it, and the law doth give it.

SHYLOCK

Most rightful judge!

PORTIA

And you must cut this flesh from off his breast;
The law allows it, and the court awards it.

SHYLOCK

Most learned judge! A sentence! Come, prepare!   300

PORTIA

Tarry[111] a little; there is something else:
This bond doth give thee here no jot of blood;
The words expressly are "a pound of flesh";
Take then thy bond, take thou thy pound of flesh,
But in the cutting it, if thou dost shed   305
One drop of Christian blood, thy lands and goods
Are (by the laws of Venice) confiscate
Unto the state of Venice.

GRATIANO

                         O upright judge! –
Mark,[112] Jew – O learned judge!

SHYLOCK

Is that the law?

185

113 *Thyself* – "You yourself".
114 *Soft!* – "Quiet! Wait a moment!"
115 *all justice* – "nothing but justice".
116 *in the substance . . . poor scruple*
(line 326) – "in the amount or a
fraction (*division*) of the twentieth
part of one little scruple". A
scruple is a measure of weight used
for medicines; it is a very small
quantity, and a twentieth part of it
is called a *grain*.

117 *turn* – "be tipped, unbalanced".
118 *estimation* – "amount".

PORTIA

Thyself[113] shalt see the act;   310
For as thou urgest justice, be assured
Thou shalt have justice more than thou desir'st.

GRATIANO

O learned judge! – Mark, Jew, a learned judge!

SHYLOCK

I take this offer then; pay the bond thrice,
And let the Christian go.

BASSANIO

Here is the money.   315

PORTIA

Soft![114]
The Jew shall have all justice;[115] soft, no haste!
He shall have nothing but the penalty.

GRATIANO

O Jew! an upright judge, a learned judge!

PORTIA

Therefore prepare thee to cut off the flesh;   320
Shed thou no blood, nor cut thou less nor more
But just a pound of flesh. If thou tak'st more
Or less than a just pound, be it but so much
As makes it light or heavy in the substance[116]
Or the division of the twentieth part   325
Of one poor scruple – nay, if the scale do turn[117]
But in the estimation[118] of a hair,
Thou diest, and all thy goods are confiscate.

119 *A second Daniel.* See note 87 and line 219 above, and lines 336–7 below.

120 *on the hip* – "at a disadvantage" *v.* note 16, p. 28.

121 *the devil ... question* – "let the devil give him the profit of it (the forfeiture); I'll not argue the case any longer".

GRATIANO

A second Daniel,[119] A Daniel, Jew ! –
Now, infidel, I have you on the hip.[120] 330

PORTIA

Why doth the Jew pause? [*To* SHYLOCK] Take thy forfeiture.

SHYLOCK

Give me my principal, and let me go.

BASSANIO

I have it ready for thee; here it is.

PORTIA

He hath refused it in the open court;
He shall have merely justice and his bond. 335

GRATIANO

A Daniel still say I, a second Daniel!
I thank thee Jew for teaching me that word.

SHYLOCK

Shall I not have barely my principal?

PORTIA

Thou shalt have nothing but the forfeiture,
To be so taken at thy peril, Jew. 340

SHYLOCK

Why then, the devil[121] give him good of it;
I 'll stay no longer question.

PORTIA

Tarry, Jew;
The law hath yet another hold on you.

122 *'gainst the which* – "against whom".

123 *contrive* – "plot".

124 *privy coffer* – "private treasury". This must mean that the property does not become public money but goes to the Duke, as head of the state, and is at his disposal.

125 *in* – "at".

126 *'gainst all other voice* – "irrespective of any other appeals"; i.e. the offender was then entirely in the Duke's power, and no one was allowed to defend him.

127 *formerly by me rehearsed* – "which I have stated just now".

128 *Down* – "Kneel".

129 *a cord,* i.e. a rope to hang by.

130 *charge* – "expense"

131 *That* – "So that".

132 *For* – "As for".

133 *Which humbleness . . . fine* – "and if you submit peaceably, it may persuade me to reduce this (the second half of your property) to a fine".

134 *for the . . . Antonio.* Portia means, apparently, that the reduction which the Duke mentioned should apply only to the property going to the state, not to the half which goes to Antonio.

135 *Nay, take my life . . .* Shylock's speech here is meant to show his, the Jew's, love of worldly goods. His property is what he lives for, and if the property is taken away he might as well give up his life also, for otherwise only misery can result.

It is enacted in the laws of Venice,
If it be proved against an alien   345
That by direct or indirect attempts
He seek the life of any citizen,
The party 'gainst the which[122] he doth contrive,[123]
Shall seize one half his goods; the other half
Comes to the privy coffer[124] of the state,   350
And the offender's life lies in[125] the mercy
Of the Duke only, 'gainst all other voice.[126]
In which predicament I say thou stand'st;
For it appears by manifest proceeding,
That indirectly, and directly too,   355
Thou hast contrived against the very life
Of the defendant; and thou hast incurred
The danger formerly by me rehearsed.[127]
Down,[128] therefore, and beg mercy of the duke.

                    GRATIANO

reflects Elizabethan audience.

Beg that thou may'st have leave to hang thyself.
And yet, thy wealth being forfeit to the state,   360
Thou hast not left the value of a cord;[129]
Therefore thou must be hanged at the state's charge.[130]

                    DUKE

That[131] thou shalt see the difference of our spirit.
I pardon thee thy life before thou ask it;
For[132] half thy wealth, it is Antonio's,   365

Mercy.

The other half comes to the general state,
Which humbleness[133] may drive unto a fine.

                    PORTIA

Ay, for the[134] state, not for Antonio.

                    SHYLOCK   *subhuman*

Nay, take my life[135] and all, pardon not that.   370
You take my house when you do take the prop

136 *So please* – "If it pleases".
137 *quit* – "remit". Antonio asks that the fine which the Duke thought of imposing (instead of the confiscation of half Shylock's goods for the state, line 368) should be remitted, i.e. Shylock should be excused from paying it.
138 *so* – "on the condition that".
139 *in use* – "in trust". Antonio will look after it until Shylock dies, and then pass it to Lorenzo. The exact purpose of this arrangement, however, is not clear; perhaps the interest on the property is to be paid to Shylock until he dies. But if it is a matter of land, Antonio's suggestion is a method of securing the ownership of land; the process at one time was that it passed through a third person, who held it until the death of its first owner, and then went to the second owner.

140 *Two things . . . more* – "Let there be two more conditions".
141 *possessed* – "possessed with".

That doth sustain my house; you take my life
When you do take the means whereby I live.

PORTIA

What mercy can you render him, Antonio?

GRATIANO

A halter gratis; nothing else, for God's sake!   375

free rope .

ANTONIO

So please[136] my lord the Duke and all the court
To quit[137] the fine for one half of his goods,
I am content; so[138] he will let me have
The other half in use,[139] to render it
Upon his death unto the gentleman
That lately stole his daughter.
Two things[140] provided more, – that for this favour
He presently become a Christian;
The other, that he do record a gift,
Here in the court, of all he dies possessed[141]
Unto his son Lorenzo and his daughter.

– Mercy .

doing Natural
thing to do .
(i.e. passing
wealth down .)   385

– importance of
money

DUKE

He shall do this, or else I do recant
The pardon that I late pronouncéd here.

PORTIA

Art thou contented, Jew? What dost thou say?

SHYLOCK

I am content.

PORTIA

Clerk, draw a deed of gift.   390

193

142 *In christening ... font* (line 396). When Shylock becomes a Christian he will have to have two godfathers. In Shakespeare's day men sitting on a jury were jokingly called "godfathers"; Gratiano wishes that Shylock had had not two but twelve "godfathers", i.e. twelve jurymen sitting on his case, who would have condemned him to hanging (on the *gallows*), not christening (at the *font*).

143 *meet* – "proper".

144 *gratify* – "pay for the services of".

145 *much bound* – "greatly indebted".

146 *in lieu whereof* – "in place of which".

147 *Three thousand ... withal* – "we gladly reward you (*cope*) for the trouble you have kindly taken (*your courteous pains*) with the three thousand ducats which were to have been handed ove to the Jew."

SHYLOCK

I pray you give me leave to go from hence;
I am not well; send the deed after me,
And I will sign it.

DUKE

Get thee gone, but do it.

GRATIANO

In christening[142] shalt thou have two godfathers;
Had I been judge, thou shouldst have had ten more,
To bring thee to the gallows, not to the font.   395

[*Exit* SHYLOCK

DUKE

Sir, I entreat you home with me to dinner.

PORTIA

I humbly do desire your grace of pardon;
I must away this night toward Padua,
And it is meet[143] I presently set forth.   400

DUKE

I am sorry that your leisure serves you not.
Antonio, gratify[144] this gentleman,
For in my mind you are much bound[145] to him.

[*Exit* DUKE *and his train*

BASSANIO

Most worthy gentleman, I and my friend
Have by your wisdom been this day acquitted   405
Of grievous penalties, in lieu whereof,[146]
Three thousand ducats[147] due unto the Jew
We freely cope your courteous pains withal.

195

148 *over and above*, i.e. more than the amount paid.

149 *I pray ... again.* Here is some more of Portia's delightful irony; there is no chance that Bassanio will know the judge when they meet again unless Portia explains who she really is.

150 *of force ... further* – "I must of necessity try again to persuade you".

151 *for your love* – "as a token of friendship". Both the gloves and the ring seem to be Bassanio's, since it is he who has pleaded so hard that Portia should take some reward. Some, however, have thought that the gloves were Antonio's. The irony is certainly more pointed if all that Portia says here is taken as being addressed to her husband; for instance, the ring in question is the one Portia gave him as a token of their love (III.ii.171–4).

ANTONIO

And stand indebted over and above[148]
In love and service to you evermore.   410

PORTIA

He is well paid that is well satisfied,
And I, delivering you, am satisfied,
And therein do account myself well paid;
My mind was never yet more mercenary.
I pray[149] you know me when we meet again;   415
I wish you well, and so I take my leave.

BASSANIO

Dear sir, of force[150] I must attempt you further;
Take some remembrance of us as a tribute,
Not as a fee. Grant me two things, I pray you:
Not to deny me, and to pardon me.   420

PORTIA

You press me far, and therefore I will yield.
Give me your gloves; I 'll wear them for your sake;
And, for your love,[151] I 'll take this ring from you.
Do not draw back your hand; I 'll take no more,
And you in love shall not deny me this!   425

BASSANIO

This ring, good sir? Alas, it is a trifle;
I will not shame myself to give you this!

PORTIA

I will have nothing else but only this,
And now methinks I have a mind to it!

BASSANIO

There 's more depends on this than on the value.   430

152 *Only for this . . . me* – "but as for this one (i.e. this particular ring) please excuse me (from giving it up to you)".

153 *You taught . . . beg.* This recalls an English proverb: "Beggars should not be choosers." Bassanio's fault is that he offers things too readily without thinking of the consequences. See note 105 above.

154 *'scuse* for *excuse* (noun).

155 *hold out enemy* – "continue to be your enemy".

156 *commandement* is to be pronounced with four syllables.

The dearest ring in Venice will I give you,
And find it out by proclamation,
Only for this[152] I pray you pardon me!

PORTIA

I see, sir, you are liberal in offers;
You taught[153] me first to beg, and now methinks   435
You teach me how a beggar should be answered.

BASSANIO

Good sir, this ring was given me by my wife,
And when she put it on, she made me vow
That I should neither sell, nor give, nor lose it.

PORTIA

That 'scuse[154] serves many men to save their gifts,   440
And if your wife be not a mad woman,
And know how well I have deserved this ring,
She would not hold out enemy[155] for ever
For giving it to me. Well, peace be with you!

              [*Exeunt* PORTIA *and* NERISSA

ANTONIO

My Lord Bassanio, let him have the ring;   445
Let his deservings and my love withal
Be valued 'gainst your wife's commandement.[156]

BASSANIO

Go, Gratiano, run and overtake him,
Give him the ring, and bring him if thou canst
Unto Antonio's house. Away, make haste.   [*Exit* GRATIANO 450
Come, you and I will thither presently,
And in the morning early will we both
Fly toward Belmont. – Come, Antonio.   [*Exeunt*

(IV.ii) Gratiano, whom Bassanio has sent with the ring, overtakes Portia and Nerissa. When the ring has been handed over, Nerissa tells Portia that she will try to get *her* ring from Gratiano.

1 *Inquire* ... *out* – "Find out where ... is".

2 *advice* – "consideration".

3 *old swearing* – "a lot of swearing".

4 *tarry* – "stay, lodge (for the night)".

Scene II. Venice. A street.

Enter PORTIA *and* NERISSA.

PORTIA

Inquire the Jew's house out;[1] give him this deed,
And let him sign it. We 'll away to-night,
And be a day before our husbands home.
This deed will be well welcome to Lorenzo!

Enter GRATIANO

GRATIANO

Fair sir, you are well o'erta'en: 5
My Lord Bassanio, upon more advice,[2]
Hath sent you here this ring, and doth entreat
Your company at dinner.

PORTIA

                    That cannot be;
His ring I do accept most thankfully,
And so I pray you tell him. Furthermore,   10
I pray you show my youth old Shylock's house.

GRATIANO

That will I do

NERISSA

            Sir, I would speak with you.
[*Aside to* PORTIA] I 'll see if I can get my husband's ring,
Which I did make him swear to keep for ever.

PORTIA

Thou may'st, I warrant. We shall have old swearing[3]   15
That they did give the rings away to men;
But we 'll outface them, and outswear them too.
Away, make haste! Thou know'st where I will tarry.[4]

NERISSA

Come, good sir, will you show me to this house?   [*Exeunt*

ACT FIVE

(v.i) It is night-time at Belmont; Lorenzo and Jessica are in the garden enjoying the night air and the moonlight. News is brought that both Portia and Bassanio are near by, and will soon be home. Lorenzo orders music to welcome them, and speaks, in words of great beauty, about the delights of music and the harmony of the universe as seen in the movement of the moon and the stars. Soon Portia and Nerissa arrive, and, in a moment, Bassanio and Gratiano with Antonio enter from the other side of the stage. After greetings have been exchanged, the matter of the rings is mentioned. The two women pretend to be very angry that the rings have been given away, and are sure, they say, that the men have given them to other women. At last Portia tells the truth, but only after a good deal of teasing. She has also brought news that three of Antonio's ships have, after all, returned safely. The play ends with Nerissa telling Lorenzo and Jessica that they will get Shylock's property, and Gratiano's promise to be faithful to *the doctor's clerk*, his wife Nerissa.

This last act has no tragic implications, and the rapid clearing-up of difficulties (the matter of the rings; Antonio's losses at sea) is in the style of pure comedy. So too is the opportunity for dramatic irony which the disguise of Portia and Nerissa as men in the court-room gives to the final explanations; this depends particularly on the confusion between men and women. But perhaps the best-loved passages here are the exchange between Lorenzo and Jessica as they look at the stars and listen to the music in the garden of Belmont.

1 *In such a night* . . . The night is so beautiful that Lorenzo and Jessica are each in turn reminded of famous incidents which took place at night. These incidents are from old stories, and at last they turn jokingly to their own case, as if Lorenzo and Jessica were also characters in a classical story.

2 *Troilus* was one of the sons of Priam, King of Troy. A famous story tells how, when Troy was being besieged by the Greeks, Troilus was in love with a faithless girl called Cressida (*Cressid,* line 6), who deserted to the Greek camp. Shakespeare wrote a play, *Troilus and Cressida,* on this story.

3 *Thisbe* was a girl of Babylon who loved her neighbour's son, a youth called Pyramus. On one occasion they agreed to meet at a certain place, but before Pyramus got there, Thisbe, who had arrived first, saw a lion which had just killed an ox, and was bloody. She ran away in fear and dropped a garment which the lion picked up and stained with blood. Pyramus, when he arrived, found the garment, and thought that Thisbe had been killed; he therefore killed himself, and when Thisbe found his body she took her own life. (Bottom and his players act this story in Shakespeare's play *A Midsummer Night's Dream.*)

Shakespeare assumed that his audience knew these stories and therefore referred to them in delightful, poetic language, but did not explain them.

204

continued on page 206

ACT FIVE

Scene I. Belmont. A green place in front of Portia's house.
Night-time.

Enter LORENZO *and* JESSICA.

LORENZO

The moon shines bright. In such a night[1] as this,
When the sweet wind did gently kiss the trees,
And they did make no noise, in such a night
Troilus[2] methinks mounted the Trojan walls,
And sighed his soul toward the Grecian tents   5
Where Cressid lay that night.

JESSICA

             In such a night
Did Thisbe[3] fearfully[4] o'ertrip[5] the dew,
And saw the lion's[6] shadow ere himself,
And ran dismayed away.

LORENZO

             In such a night
Stood Dido[7] with a willow in her hand   10
Upon the wild sea banks, and waft[8] her love
To come again[9] to Carthage.

JESSICA

             In such a night
Medea[10] gathered the enchanted herbs
That did renew old Æson.

LORENZO

             In such a night
Did Jessica steal[11] from the wealthy Jew,   15

4 *fearfully* – "in fear".

5 *o'ertrip* – "step lightly over".

6 *the lion's . . . himself* – "the shape of the lion before (she saw) her lover (Pyramus)".

7 *Dido* was queen of the city of Carthage in North Africa. Virgil tells the story of her love for Aeneas, a noble Roman, who deserted her to seek the new home which the gods had promised him. A spray of willow was a sign of forsaken love.

8 *waft* for *wafted* – "waved".

9 *again* – "back".

10 *Medea* was the daughter of the King of Colchis, and it was she who helped Jason win the golden fleece (see note 127, p. 126 above). Having (like Jessica) stolen her father's treasure, she ran away to Greece with her lover, and there she made a medicine of magic herbs which restored Jason's father, the aged Aeson, to youth and vigour. The mention of Medea reminds Lorenzo of Jessica.

11 *steal* here means both "leave in secret" and "take what was not her own".

12 *unthrift* – "wasteful"; she spent money very freely on the journey, as Tubal told Shylock: "Your daughter spent in Genoa, as I heard, one night, fourscore ducats." (III.i.88–9)

13 *Stealing* – "winning by means of the charm of love"; Morocco speaks of stealing Portia's thoughts (II.i.12). This is a further meaning of the word *steal*, which they have already played on.

14 *out-night you* – "give more examples of what happened 'in such a night' than you can".

15 *did nobody come* – "if nobody were coming".

16 *footing* – "footsteps".

17 *holy crosses;* these were crosses set up by the roadside for travellers to pray at.

And with an unthrift[12] love did run from Venice
As far as Belmont.

JESSICA

       In such a night
Did young Lorenzo swear he loved her well,
Stealing[13] her soul with many vows of faith,
And ne'er a true one.

LORENZO

       In such a night   20
Did pretty Jessica, like a little shrew,
Slander her love, and he forgave it her.

JESSICA

I would out-night you[14] did nobody come:[15]
But hark, I hear the footing[16] of a man.

Enter STEPHANO

LORENZO

Who comes so fast in silence of the night?   25

STEPHANO

A friend!

LORENZO

A friend! what friend? your name, I pray you, friend?

STEPHANO

Stephano is my name, and I bring word
My mistress will before the break of day
Be here at Belmont. She doth stray about   30
By holy crosses,[17] where she kneels and prays
For happy wedlock hours.

LORENZO

       Who comes with her?

18 *a holy hermit.* Portia's story as to why she left Belmont was that she was going to a monastery, "To live in prayer and contemplation" for a while (III.iv.27).

19 *Sola, . . . sola!* This imitates the sound of the horn which the messenger sounded as he brought the post; Launcelot announces himself as *a post* in line 46 below.

20 *Leave hollowing man; here! –* "Stop shouting, man; (I am here!"

21 *post* – "messenger".

22 *horn,* i.e. the horn blown by the post when he arrives; but Launcelot is probably punning on *the horn of plenty,* a goat's horn from which pour fruits, flowers and corn, seen in pictures as a symbol of plenty.

23 *let 's in* – "let us go indoors".

24 *expect* – "await".

his horn full of good news [22]

STEPHANO

None but a holy hermit[18] and her maid.
I pray you, is my master yet returned?

LORENZO

He is not, nor we have not heard from him. –   35
But go we in, I pray thee, Jessica,
And ceremoniously let us prepare
Some welcome for the mistress of the house.

Enter LAUNCELOT.

LAUNCELOT

Sola,[19] sola, wo ha, ho! sola, sola!

LORENZO

Who calls?   40

LAUNCELOT

Sola! did you see Master Lorenzo? Master Lorenzo, sola,
sola!

LORENZO

Leave hollowing man; here![20]

LAUNCELOT

Sola! where, where?

LORENZO

Here!   45

LAUNCELOT

Tell him there 's a post[21] come from my master, with his
horn[22] full of good news; my master will be here ere morning.

[*Exit*

LORENZO

Sweet soul, let 's in,[23] and there expect[24] their coming.
And yet no matter; why should we go in?
My friend Stephano, signify, I pray you,   50
Within the house, your mistress is at hand,
And bring your music forth into the air.

[*Exit* STEPHANO

25 *How sweet the moonlight . . .* Shakespeare is here, as elsewhere, inspired to write the most beautiful poetry on thoughts concerned with music. Lorenzo has told the musicians to prepare to welcome Portia with music when she returns. But he and Jessica will not go indoors to listen to it; instead they sit outside in the quiet of the moonlit night and let the music drift over to them. The beauty and order of Shakespeare's words make a music of their own. At the end of the passage, Lorenzo looks at the stars and thinks of the "music of the spheres", the heavenly harmony which is too fine for mortal ears to hear.

26 *Become the touches . . . harmony* – "are fitting for the notes (*touches*) of sweet harmony".

27 *patens* – "small shallow dishes". In Shakespeare's day people thought of the stars as round shining objects, each moving within a limited space in the sky, a "sphere" in which it was "inlaid". But for Lorenzo the image suggested is also of a floor with golden points let into it.

28 *the smallest orb . . . angel sings.* This passage refers to the "spheres" which the stars were thought to move in: the circles of the stars were imagined as touching each other, so that as each moved a musical note was produced. And since the stars did not strike one another, but each kept to its own "sphere", a harmony of motion gave a harmony of sound; this was called the "music of the spheres". Human beings could not hear it, however, because they were not awake or sensitive enough to do so. Nevertheless, many people have been moved with the idea that there is a harmony of motion in the universe, of which musical harmony is a fitting image; (*orb* – "star").

29 *Still quiring . . . cherubins* – "singing (*quiring*) continuously (*still*) to the cherubins with sight ever young".

30 *Such harmony . . . it* (line 64) – "The ability to appreciate such music rests in the souls of immortals (such as the cherubin); but while this earthly, decaying clothing of ours (our bodies, the *muddy vesture of decay*) completely closes the soul in, we cannot hear it (the music)".

31 *wake Diana* – "celebrate Diana", goddess of the moon.

32 *touches* – "notes", as played by the fingers.

33 *spirits are* – "mind is".

34 *do but note* – "just notice".

35 *unhandled* – "untrained".

36 *Fetching mad bounds* – "leaping up madly".

37 *perchance* – "by chance".

38 *mutual stand* – "a stop common to all", i.e. they all stop together.

39 *Therefore the poet . . . trees* – "For this reason the poet made up the story of how Orpheus caused trees . . . to follow him". Shakespeare took many hints of classical stories from Ovid, and perhaps Ovid is the poet mentioned here. In his book *Metamorphoses* (x and xi) he tells how Orpheus, a poet, was given a lyre by Apollo, and learned to play on it so enchantingly that not only the wild beasts but even trees and rocks followed him as he played.

40 *naught so stockish* – "there is nothing so insensitive".

41 *But music . . . nature* – "that music does not temporarily change its nature".

and as Stephano leaves tranquility is reestablished.

How sweet the moonlight[25] sleeps upon this bank!
Here will we sit, and let the sounds of music
Creep in our ears; soft stillness and the night
Become the touches[26] of sweet harmony.
Sit, Jessica. Look how the floor of heaven
Is thick inlaid with patens[27] of bright gold;
There's not the smallest orb[28] which thou behold'st
But in his motion like an angel sings,
Still quiring[29] to the young-eyed cherubins;   60
Such harmony[30] is in immortal souls,
But whilst this muddy vesture of decay
Doth grossly close it in, we cannot hear it

association with the harmony of Belmont

power of music.

Enter Musicians.

Come, ho! and wake Diana[31] with a hymn!
With sweetest touches[32] pierce your mistress' ear,   65
And draw her home with music.

Jessica's educated

[*Music*

JESSICA

am never merry when I hear sweet music.

away from 'music loathing' Shylock into civilised christian life.

LORENZO

The reason is your spirits[33] are attentive;
For do but note[34] a wild and wanton herd
Or race of youthful and unhandled[35] colts
Fetching mad bounds,[36] bellowing and neighing loud,
Which is the hot condition of their blood.
If they but hear perchance[37] a trumpet sound,
Or any air of music touch their ears,   75
You shall perceive them make a mutual stand,[38]
Their savage eyes turned to a modest gaze
By the sweet power of music. Therefore the poet[39]
Did feign that Orpheus drew trees, stones, and floods,
Since naught so stockish,[40] hard, and full of rage,   80
But music[41] for the time doth change his nature.

42 *spoils* – "acts of theft and destruction".

43 *affections* – "character".

44 *Erebus* is described in ancient Greek stories as a dark place in the underworld.

45 *main of waters* – "ocean".

46 *music* – "musicians".

47 *Nothing ... respect* – (perhaps) "nothing is perfectly good, I see, but good only in relation to the attendant circumstances". What Portia seems to be saying is that nothing is in itself completely satisfying, but its effect depends on the circumstances; however perfect the music is in the day-time, it sounds better at night.

48 *When neither is attended* – "when each is by itself". The difference of quality in the songs of these birds is best heard when they are together; in the same way the candle was a powerful light until it could be compared with the moon.

49 *The nightingale* sings at night when all the other birds are silent, and its song can therefore be heard at its full beauty, and not compared with the songs of other birds.

the young-eyed cherubins [29]

The man that hath no music in himself,
Nor is not moved with concord of sweet sounds,
Is fit for treasons, stratagems, and spoils;[42]
The motions of his spirit are dull as night,   85
And his affections[43] dark as Erebus;[44]
Let no such man be trusted. – Mark the music.

Enter PORTIA *and* NERISSA, *at a distance from the others.*

PORTIA

That light we see is burning in my hall.
How far that little candle throws his beams!
So shines a good deed in a naughty world.   90

NERISSA

When the moon shone, we did not see the candle.

PORTIA

So doth the greater glory dim the less;
A substitute shines brightly as a king
Until a king be by, and then his state
Empties itself, as doth an inland brook   95
Into the main of waters.[45] – Music! hark!

middle class ideal

NERISSA

It is your music,[46] madam, of the house.

Belmont philosophy.

PORTIA

Nothing[47] is good, I see, without respect;
Methinks it sounds much sweeter than by day.

NERISSA

Silence bestows that virtue on it, madam.   100

PORTIA

The crow doth sing as sweetly as the lark
When neither is attended;[48] and I think
The nightingale,[49] if she should sing by day,
When every goose is cackling, would be thought

50 *by season seasoned are* – "are appreciated (*seasoned*) by happening at a favourable time (*by season*)".

51 *the moon . . . Endymion.* Endymion was a beautiful young man who, according to an old Greek story, won even the cold heart of Diana, the moon goddess. She put him to eternal sleep so that she could lie by his side and kiss him. Thoughts of Endymion and the moon draw attention to Lorenzo and Jessica sitting entranced on the bank.

52 *Which speed . . .* – "who (the husbands) journey, fare".

53 *before,* i.e. in front of the husbands.

54 *they take . . . absent hence* – "they make no remarks at all about our being away from home".

55 *tucket,* a series of loud notes on a trumpet. It seems that important people had their own special trumpet calls and could be recognized by them.

56 *tell-tales* – "tellers of secrets". He promises he will tell no one that Portia and Nerissa have been away from home. Portia now hears that Bassanio and his friends are near by, and she quickly changes the subject: she remarks on how bright the night is, and Bassanio overhears her and takes up the subject.

No better a musician than the wren!
How many things by season seasoned are[50]
To their right praise, and true perfection!
Peace! – how the moon sleeps with Endymion,[51]
And would not be awaked!   [*Music ceases*

                    LORENZO
                    That is the voice,
Or I am much deceived, of Portia.   110

                    PORTIA

He knows me as the blind man knows the cuckoo –
By the bad voice!

                    LORENZO
                    Dear lady, welcome home!

                    PORTIA

We have been praying for our husbands' welfare,
Which speed,[52] we hope, the better for our words.
Are they returned?

                    LORENZO
                    Madam, they are not yet;   115
But there is come a messenger before[53]
To signify their coming.

                    PORTIA
                    Go in, Nerissa.
Give order to my servants that they take[54]
No note at all of our being absent hence;
Nor you, Lorenzo; Jessica, nor you.   [*A tucket[55] sounds* 120

                    LORENZO

Your husband is at hand; I hear his trumpet;
We are no tell-tales,[56] madam; fear you not.

                    215

57 *sick*, and therefore pale in the face.

58 *hold day ... Antipodes* – "enjoy daytime at the same time as the other side of the earth".

59 *in absence ... sun* – "when the sun is not shining", i.e. at night-time.

60 *light* – "immoral".

61 *never be ... me* – "may Bassanio never be (made *heavy*, sad) on my account".

62 *God sort all* – "let God decide everything", "leave everything to God".

63 *in all sense* – "(probably) in every sense" (of the word *bound*). Portia plays on *bound* meaning "obliged" and, in the next line, *bound* meaning "arrested". But the phrase *in all sense* may here mean "on every account".

64 *It*, i.e. This welcome.

65 *I scant ... courtesy* – "I give little in the way of polite words". Words are simply breath (*breathing*); Antonio's welcome will be shown in deeds, not just words.

PORTIA

This night methinks is but the daylight sick;[57]
It looks a little paler – 't is a day
Such as the day is when the sun is hid.   125

Enter BASSANIO, ANTONIO, GRATIANO, *and their*
followers.

BASSANIO

We should hold day[58] with the Antipodes,
If you would walk in absence[59] of the sun.

PORTIA

Let me *give* light, but let me not *be* light,[60]
For a light wife doth make a heavy husband,
And never be[61] Bassanio so for me. –   130
But God sort all![62] You are welcome home, my lord.

BASSANIO

I thank you, madam. Give welcome to my friend;
This is the man, this is Antonio,
To whom I am so infinitely bound.

PORTIA

You should in all sense[63] be much bound to him,   135
For, as I hear, he was much bound for you.

ANTONIO

No more than I am well acquitted of.

PORTIA

[*To* ANTONIO] Sir, you are very welcome to our house.
It[64] must appear in other ways than words;
Therefore I scant[65] this breathing courtesy.   140

66 *it*, i.e. the ring which Nerissa said she would try to get back from her husband (IV.ii.13–14).

67 *gelt* – "made to lose his sex as a man". The judge's clerk was in fact a woman.

68 *posy* – "motto". This motto was usually a line of verse engraved, for instance, inside a ring or on a knife.

69 *cutler's poetry* – "the poetry written by the knife-maker".

70 *leave me not* – "do not part with me". The *posy* refers both to the ring and also to the woman who gave it.

71 *What talk you* – "Why do you talk".

72 *Though* – "Even though".

73 *respective* – "careful".

74 *The clerk ... had it* – "the clerk who had it (the ring) will never have a beard", i.e. will never grow to be a man. The irony of this and the following lines is delightfully amusing: Nerissa was, of course, the clerk, and she will certainly never grow to be a man. The touch is continued in "*No higher than thyself*" in line 162.

75 *and if* – "if".

76 *scrubbed* – "undergrown".

GRATIANO

[*To* NERISSA] By yonder moon I swear you do me wrong;
In faith I gave it[66] to the judge's clerk
Would he were gelt[67] that had it for my part,
Since you do take it, love, so much at heart.

PORTIA

A quarrel, ho, already! What 's the matter?   145

GRATIANO

About a hoop of gold, a paltry ring
That she did give me, whose posy[68] was
For all the world like cutler's poetry[69]
Upon a knife: "Love me, and leave me not."[70]

NERISSA

What talk you[71] of the posy or the value?   150
You swore to me when I did give it you
That you would wear it till your hour of death,
And that it should lie with you in your grave.
Though[72] not for me, yet for your vehement oaths
You should have been respective[73] and have kept it.   155
Gave it a judge's clerk! no, God 's my judge,
The clerk[74] will ne'er wear hair on 's face that had it.

GRATIANO

He will, and if[75] he live to be a man.

NERISSA

Ay, if a woman live to be a man. ——   *accusing giving to a woman*

GRATIANO

Now, by this hand, I gave it to a youth,   160
A kind of boy, a little scrubbéd[76] boy,
No higher than thyself, the judge's clerk,

77 *leave* – "part with". Portia now turns attention to Bassanio. As the judge, she finally persuaded Bassanio to give his ring to her, and now she knows very well that he no longer has it.

78 *the wealth ... masters* – "all the wealth that the world possesses".

79 *An 't were* – "if it were".

80 *I were best* – "it would be best for me".

81 *took ... writing* – "went to some trouble over the writing".

A prating boy that begged it as a fee.
I could not for my heart deny it him.

PORTIA

You were to blame, I must be plain with you,   165
To part so slightly with your wife's first gift,
A thing stuck on with oaths upon your finger,
And so riveted with faith unto your flesh.
I gave my love a ring, and made him swear
Never to part with it, and here he stands: 170
I dare be sworn for him he would not leave[77] it,
Nor pluck it from his finger, for the wealth[78]
That the world masters. Now, in faith, Gratiano,
You give your wife too unkind a cause of grief;
An 't were[79] to me I should be mad at it.   175

BASSANIO

[*Aside*] Why, I were best[80] to cut my left hand off,
And swear I lost the ring defending it.

GRATIANO

My Lord Bassanio gave his ring away
Unto the judge that begged it, and indeed
Deserved it too; and then the boy, his clerk,   180
That took[81] some pains in writing, he begged mine,
And neither man nor master would take aught
But the two rings.

PORTIA

What ring gave you, my lord?
Not that, I hope, which you received of me.

BASSANIO

If I could add a lie unto a fault,   185
I would deny it; but you see my finger
Hath not the ring upon it; it is gone.

82 *conceive* – "fully understand". Bassanio ends five of his lines with *the ring* so as to emphasize the genuineness of his excuses. Portia takes up this form of words in her reply.

83 *contain* – "keep".

84 *What man ... ceremony?* (line 205) – "What man is there so unreasonable – if you had wanted to defend the ring with any show of zeal – and so lacking in moderation (*wanted the modesty*) that he would have insisted upon (*urge*) (the giving up of) the thing kept as a formal symbol of faith (*a ceremony*)?" The ring is a symbol of the married state.

85 *a civil doctor*, i.e. a doctor of civil law. (Civil law is confined to questions of private rights.) But *civil* may here mean "polite, agreeable" as well.

86 *suffered* – "allowed".

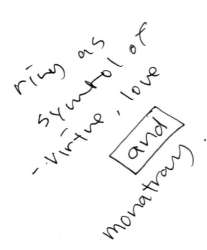

ring as symbol of
Symbol love
– virtue, love
and
monatrany).

PORTIA

Even so void is your false heart of truth.
By heaven I will ne'er come in your bed
Until I see the ring!

NERISSA

[*To* GRATIANO]   Nor I in yours   190
Till I again see mine!

BASSANIO

            Sweet Portia,
If you did know to whom I gave the ring,
If you did know for whom I gave the ring,
And would conceive[82] for what I gave the ring,
And how unwillingly I left the ring,   195
When nought would be accepted but the ring,
You would abate the strength of your displeasure.

PORTIA

If you had known the virtue of the ring,
Or half her worthiness that gave the ring,
Or your own honour to contain[83] the ring,   200
You would not then have parted with the ring.
What man[84] is there so much unreasonable,
If you had pleased to have defended it
With any terms of zeal, wanted the modesty
To urge the thing held as a ceremony?   205
Nerissa teaches me what to believe:
I 'll die for 't, but some woman had the ring!

BASSANIO

No, by my honour, madam, by my soul,   210
No woman had it, but a civil doctor,[85]
Which did refuse three thousand ducats of me,
And begged the ring; the which I did deny him,
And suffered[86] him to go displeased away,

87 *held up* – "defended".

88 *I was beset with ... courtesy* – "I was deeply concerned with considerations of shame (at not giving what was asked) and courtesy (general good behaviour)".

89 *besmear* – "stain".

90 *candles of the night,* an image for the stars.

91 *liberal* – both (1) "free in giving", and (2) "loose in behaviour".

92 *Lie ... home* – "Do not spend a single night away from home".

93 *Argus* was the "all-seeing one" in Greek legends. He had a hundred eyes, some of which were always open. But Hermes, at the command of Zeus, managed to put him to sleep by playing to him on the flute, and then cut off his head.

94 *yet mine own* – "still mine"; Portia has not broken her word as Bassanio has done.

95 *well advised* – "very careful".

96 *take* – "catch".

Even he that had held up[87] the very life
Of my dear friend. What should I say, sweet lady?
I was enforced to send it after him;   215
I was beset with[88] shame and courtesy;
My honour would not let ingratitude
So much besmear[89] it. Pardon me, good lady,
For by these blessèd candles of the night,[90]
Had you been there, I think you would have begged   220
The ring of me to give the worthy doctor.

PORTIA

Let not that doctor e'er come near my house.
Since he hath got the jewel that I loved,
And that which you did swear to keep for me,
I will become as liberal[91] as you;   225
I 'll not deny him anything I have,
No, not my body, nor my husband's bed;
Know him I shall, I am well sure of it.
Lie[92] not a night from home. Watch me like Argus;[93]
If you do not, if I be left alone,   230
Now by mine honour, which is yet mine own,[94]
I 'll have that doctor for my bedfellow.

NERISSA

And I his clerk; therefore be well advised[95]
How you do leave me to mine own protection.

GRATIANO

Well, do you so; let not me take[96] him then,   235
For if I do, I 'll mar the young clerk's pen.

ANTONIO

I am th' unhappy subject of these quarrels.

PORTIA

Sir, grieve not you; you are welcome notwithstanding.

97 *Mark you but that!* – "Just notice that!"

98 *an oath of credit* – "an oath to be believed, an oath indeed".

99 *for his wealth* – "to his advantage".

100 *Which* – "and this (lending)".

101 *Had quite miscarried* – "would have gone completely wrong".

BASSANIO

Portia, forgive me this enforcéd wrong,
And, in the hearing of these many friends, 240
I swear to thee, even by thine own fair eyes,
Wherein I see myself –

PORTIA

       Mark you but that![97]
In both my eyes he doubly sees himself;
In each eye one; swear by your double self,
And there's an oath of credit.[98]

BASSANIO

      Nay, but hear me. 245
Pardon this fault, and by my soul I swear
I never more will break an oath with thee.

ANTONIO

I once did lend my body for his wealth,[99]
Which,[100] but for him that had your husband's ring,
Had quite miscarried.[101] I dare be bound again, 250
My soul upon the forfeit, that your lord
Will never more break faith advisedly.

PORTIA

Then you shall be his surety. Give him this,
And bid him keep it better than the other. [*She gives* ANTONIO
  a ring]

ANTONIO

Here, Lord Bassanio, swear to keep this ring. 255

BASSANIO

By heaven it is the same I gave the doctor!

PORTIA

I had it of him; pardon me, Bassanio,
For by this ring the doctor lay with me.

227

102 *In lieu of this* – "in return for this (ring)". She is giving Gratiano back his ring.

103 *this is like ... enough!* – "this is like repairing roads in the summertime, when (*where*) they are already in good condition!" It is not clear what Gratiano means by this; he is probably implying that his and Bassanio's excuses and explanations about the rings are a waste of time, because their wives have been unfaithful, as it appears, and are even more to blame than the men are. As with the roads, this is making repairs when repairs are unnecessary

104 *grossly* – "coarsely".

105 *even but now returned* – "have only just returned".

106 *soon* – "at once".

107 *suddenly* – "unexpectedly".

108 *chancéd on* – "happened to get".

NERISSA

And pardon me, my gentle Gratiano,
For that same scrubbèd boy, the doctor's clerk,   260
In lieu of[102] this, last night did lie with me.

GRATIANO

Why this is like[103] the mending of highways
In summer, where the ways are fair enough!
What, are we cuckolds ere we have deserved it?

PORTIA

Speak not so grossly.[104] You are all amazed;   265
Here is a letter; read it at your leisure;
It comes from Padua, from Bellario.
There you shall find that Portia was the doctor,
Nerissa there her clerk. Lorenzo here
Shall witness I set forth as soon as you,   270
And even but now returned;[105] I have not yet
Entered my house. Antonio, you are welcome,
And I have better news in store for you
Than you expect. Unseal this letter soon;[106]
There you shall find three of your argosies   275
Are richly come to harbour suddenly.[107]
You shall not know by what strange accident
I chancéd on[108] this letter

ANTONIO

I am dumb!

BASSANIO

Were you the doctor, and I knew you not?

GRATIANO

Were you the clerk that is to make me cuckold?   280

NERISSA

Ay, but the clerk that never means to do it,
Unless he live until he be a man.

109 *living* – "possessions".

110 *road,* place where ships anchor off shore.

111 *How now* – "And how about you".

112 *without a fee,* i.e. the money a clerk would charge for his services.

113 *manna* – The Bible (*Exodus* xvi. 14–21) tells how the Israelites complained when they had nothing to eat, and how God sent them "small round things" which they picked up from the ground and ate like bread. These they called *manna.* Lorenzo and Jessica have got through their money very quickly while they were in Genoa and Shylock's wealth is therefore as welcome to them as food is to starving people.

114 *charge us . . . inter'gatories* – "there we will answer upon oath (*charge us*) a series of questions (interrogatories)". Portia has, for the moment, slipped back into the legal language she used so sucessfully in court.

115 *So sore* – "so deeply".

BASSANIO

Sweet doctor, you shall be my bedfellow;
When I am absent then lie with my wife. *virtue, spirit*

ANTONIO

Sweet lady, you have given me life and living;[109]   285
For here I read for certain that my ships
Are safely come to road.[110]   *means to live*

PORTIA

How now,[111] Lorenzo?
My clerk hath some good comforts too for you.

NERISSA

Ay, and I 'll give them him without a fee.[112]
There do I give to you and Jessica,   290
From the rich Jew, a special deed of gift,
After his death, of all he dies possessed of.

LORENZO

Fair ladies, you drop manna[113] in the way
Of starvéd people.

PORTIA

It is almost morning,
And yet I am sure you are not satisfied   295
Of these events at full. Let us go in,
And charge us[114] there upon inter'gatories,
And we will answer all things faithfully.

GRATIANO

Let it be so; the first inter'gatory
That my Nerissa shall be sworn on is,   300
Whether till the next night she had rather stay,
Or go to bed now, being two hours to day;
But were the day come, I should wish it dark
Till I were couching with the doctor's clerk.
Well, while I live I 'll fear no other thing   305
So sore[115] as keeping safe Nerissa's ring.   [*Exeunt*

231

Final scene

restores comic, back to orde[r]

sense of harmony is estaflis[h]

note — Universal happiness.
- Lorenzo's poetic value
- Portia's wit
- the parallel mention of
  economic / virtuous.

the fact the scene happens
in Belmont and discussio[n]
is very ideal.

HINTS TO EXAMINATION CANDIDATES

This section is intended to offer some help to candidates who are studying *The Merchant of Venice* for such examinations as School Certificate or G.C.E. Ordinary Level, and who are working alone. Actual questions from London papers are used as examples to show the kinds of question that may be found on most papers for examinations at this stage.

You will see, firstly, that you must know the story of the play in some detail. Secondly, you must give yourself practice in reading the questions carefully and answering exactly what is asked; *do not expect to find on any paper a question that you have already answered.* Thirdly, you must train yourself to write quickly enough to finish the work in the time allowed (30 minutes for each of these sample questions). Do not waste time, for example, in copying out the question.

See to it that you know beforehand which kinds of question you *must* do and what you *may* do. For some examinations (e.g. London) you must do one "context" question and you may also do an essay question on the set play; for others you may have some choice between "context" and essay questions. Note that the quotations appearing on the examination paper may not correspond in every detail, e.g. punctuation, to the version given in the text in this book.

"Context" Questions

Sample questions from London University G.C.E., Ordinary Level, Summer 1960.

Choose ONE of the following passages and answer the questions below it.

EITHER—

(i)

O that estates, degrees, and offices,
Were not derived corruptly, and that clear honour
Were purchased by the merit of the wearer.

How many then should cover that stand bare?
How many be commanded that command?   5
How much low peasantry would then be gleaned
From the true seed of honour? And how much honour
Picked from the chaff and ruin of the times,
To be new-varnished? Well but to my choice.
  Who chooseth me shall get as much as he deserves.   10

(a) Who speaks these lines and on what occasion?

(b) Where does the speaker read the last line of the passage; what has
he said previously to show that this line makes an especial appeal to
him?

(c) What is meant by "gleaned from the true seed of honour" (ll. 6–7)
and "O that estates, degrees, and offices, were not derived corruptly."
(ll. 1–2)?

(d) What does the speaker choose when it comes to his "choice" (l. 9)?
What does his choice tell us about his character?

(e) Mention *two* consequences which follow the speaker's choice.

OR

(ii)

Gratiano. A second Daniel, a Daniel, Jew.
  Now infidel I have you on the hip.

Portia. Why doth the Jew pause? Take thy forfeiture.

Shylock. Give me my principal, and let me go.

Bassanio. I have it ready for thee, here it is.   5

Portia. He hath refused it in the open court.
  He shall have merely justice and his bond.

Gratiano. A Daniel still say I, a second Daniel –
  I thank thee Jew for teaching me that word.

Shylock. Shall I not have barely my principal?   10

234

(a) Where does this episode occur? Say *briefly* what is taking place.

(b) Portia asks " Why doth the Jew pause?" (l. 3). What was Shylock hesitating to do? Give *one* reason which made him pause.

(c) What was the "principal" (l. 4)? What offer had Bassanio made earlier, relating to this "principal"?

(d) What does Gratiano mean by "I have you on the hip" (l. 2)? Refer briefly to an earlier passage in which the same metaphor is used by Shylock.

(e) What is Gratiano alluding to when he says "A second Daniel" (l. 1)? Give one other instance from this scene of his taunting of Shylock.

NOTES ON POSSIBLE ANSWERS

(i)

(a) The Prince of Arragon; at Portia's house in Belmont when he is about to make his choice of the caskets.

(b) On the silver casket; that he believes he genuinely deserves the best, and there is no point in pretending otherwise.

(c) "picked out, like chaff from corn, from those who are truly the children of noble parents."

"I wish that places of high rank and social standing and important positions in the government were not obtained unworthily."

(d) The silver casket. In assuming that he deserves Portia he shows himself too proud.

(e) He finds inside this casket the portrait of an idiot, but keeps his oath to leave at once without saying anything further.

Note that a good deal of accurate information is necessary here. Write as simply and shortly as possible. Number the sections carefully. See that you have not left out any parts of the section, e.g. (b) what has he said, etc., (d) his character. For (c) keep the inverted commas of the question and explain the meaning in a phrase or sentence which could be fitted grammatically into the passage.

(a) In a court of justice in Venice; Shylock is claiming his right to receive from Antonio the penalty agreed between them, even though Portia as the judge has set him impossible conditions.

(b) To cut a pound of flesh from nearest Antonio's heart. If he were to shed one drop of Antonio's blood he would lose his own possessions and life.

(c) Three thousand ducats; to pay to Shylock twice the sum.

(d) "I have you at a disadvantage, as if, in wrestling, I have you in the right position to throw you down." When asked to lend the ducats, and just before suggesting his "merry" bond, Shylock says quietly to himself how much he hates Antonio and how, if he can catch him once upon the hip, he will "feed fat" the grudge he bears him.

(e) To a story in the Bible about the trial of Susanna, when Daniel, a wise young man acting as judge, was able to turn against the Elders their own words of accusation; so Portia has turned against Shylock the words of his bond. Also to Shylock's praise of Portia, earlier in this scene, as "A Daniel come to judgement". When all Shylock's possessions are forfeited, Gratiano taunts him with not having even the cost of a rope left to hang himself.

Notes: In (a) note the instruction *briefly*. Do not give information which will be required in answer to (b), (c), etc. Keep the inverted commas in (d), so that you will write "I have you ..." and not "He had him ...".

ESSAY QUESTIONS

Specimen questions from London University G.C.E., Ordinary Level, Summer 1960.

1. Give a concise account of the last act of the play, in which Portia returns from Venice to Belmont, referring to (a) the action, (b) the setting, and (c) the dialogue.

2. Compare the aspects of the character of Shylock shown in (*a*) his first appearance in the play and his conversation with Bassanio and Antonio, and (*b*) the Trial Scene.

3. Referring to his actions and speeches, write a detailed character sketch of Bassanio. Discuss *briefly* whether, in your opinion, he is worthy of Antonio's great friendship.

General hints on essay questions:

Make *brief notes* before you begin to write. Remember that you will certainly not have time to write out the whole essay in rough and then copy it out later. Plan carefully: the way in which the question is arranged will tell you how to plan your answer.

Any quotations given should be short; do not waste time on long quotations of ten or twenty lines; it is more important to show that you yourself can write simply and clearly. When quoting poetry, quote in lines and begin the quotation about one inch from the left-hand margin. The quotations given should fit grammatically into your own sentences.

Question 1.

Plan and Material: Remember that Act V begins with the talk of Lorenzo and Jessica in the moonlit garden. Consider into how many sections the *account* is best divided, e.g. (1) the talk of Lorenzo and Jessica: (2) the return of Portia and Nerissa followed by that of Bassanio, Antonio and Gratiano; (3) the episode of the rings.

Arrangement: Since there will not be time to deal fully with (*a*) *action*, (*b*) *setting* and (*c*) *dialogue* for all three sections, it will be best to decide which of these are most important for each. In (1) the *setting* is important and the *dialogue* also is full of poetry; in (2) the *action* is important: Portia and Nerissa have arrived home first and are able to give instructions that no-one shall tell tales about their absence; it will probably be necessary to leave out all mention of the jokes of this section so as to leave enough space for (3); in (3) the *dialogue* is full of wit and humour and the *action* is brought to a satisfactory end: the men are told who played the parts of the doctor and his clerk; Antonio has three ships safely returned; Lorenzo and Jessica are to be Shylock's heirs.

You will see that you have much to write: begin at once, without any introduction, e.g.:

The moon shines brightly as Lorenzo and Jessica, in the garden of Portia's house, remind each other of famous lovers of earlier times. News is brought that both Portia and Bassanio will be home before dawn, and Lorenzo orders music to welcome them. He describes the starry sky (give a phrase or line or two of quotation) and speaks of the sweetness of the music (short quotation or paraphrase).

Portia is glad to see the light burning in her hall and enjoys the welcoming music. She asks Lorenzo at once (what?) and gives orders that. . . . As soon as Bassanio arrives, she jokes about a wife of uncertain loyalty (quote, if possible), knowing that she is soon to reproach her husband for giving away the ring which she has given him.

Nerissa is already teasing Gratiano . . . (continue with three or four good points, and say briefly how this episode ends). The action of the play is now to be concluded. Portia tells . . . (include the three pieces of information given above).

Question 2

Plan and Material: Compare means "to set side by side so as to note similarities and differences". Make *very short* notes *in two columns* before you begin your answer. These notes are for your own use and not for the examiner to mark, but they will remind you that whatever points you choose for (*a*) – Shylock's first appearance – must be discussed also when you write on (*b*) – Shylock's character as shown in the Trial Scene. Try to find at least three or four good points, as suggested in the notes below. These notes are, of course, set out at greater length than yours would be.

(a) *first appearance*	(b) *in Trial Scene*
1. (i) S. *seems* to think slowly: "I think I may take his bond." (ii) Pretends to be rather forgetful: "I had forgot – three months; you told me so." (iii) Is not very clear in his argument when he tells the story of Jacob and Laban.	1. (i) Thinks quickly. Argues clearly and firmly. (ii) He claims only what is legal. If Venice will not give him what is lawful, let the city lose its good name for justice. (iii) As the Christians buy their slaves, so he has bought Antonio's flesh.
2. He pretends that his bond is a jest: what is the good of a pound of a man's flesh?	2. He prefers a "weight of carrion flesh" to three thousand ducats.
3. Much of his personal hatred of Antonio is kept hidden: "How like a fawning publican he looks!"	3. Speaks openly of the "lodged hate" and "certain loathing" he feels for A.
4. His dislike of Christians is shown: he will not eat, drink or pray with them.	4. He would rather that his daughter had married any man of Jewish faith than a Christian.
5. He speaks with genuine feeling of Antonio's bad treatment of him: Many a time and oft In the Rialto you have rated me . . . and he asks "Hath a dog money?"	5. Makes little complaint and asks for no pity: "Give me my principal, and let me go"; "I am content." Speaks with dignity even in a time of bodily weakness: "I am not well; send the deed after me."

Arrangement: It is possible to write your answer in two sections with (a) *first appearance* followed by (b) *Trial Scene*, but it is easier to keep to the requirements of the question if you compare (*a*) 1 with (*b*) 1 and then (*a*) 2 with (*b*) 2, etc. Begin at once, without any introduction, e.g.:

At his first appearance in the play Shylock seems to think slowly, but in the Trial Scene he can think quickly and argue firmly.

GLOSSARY

This glossary explains all those words in the play which are used in Modern English as they were in Shakespeare's day, but are not among the 3,000 most-used words in the language.

The notes opposite the text explain words which are *not* used in Modern English. In these notes it has been necessary to use one or two words which are also outside the 3,000-word list; these are included in this glossary.

Explanations in the glossary are given entirely within the chosen list of words; only the meaning of the word as used in the text or notes is normally given.

v. = verb; n. = noun.

A

abate, to make less.

abject, wretched.

acquit, to declare that a person is not guilty of a wrong he has been accused of.

adversary, an enemy.

advisedly, on purpose.

agitation, anxiety.

alien, a foreigner.

alight, to get down (from a horse).

allay, to make less.

aloof, at a distance.

ambassador, a person sent to act for someone else.

amiss, wrongly.

amity, friendship.

amorous, loving.

antipodes, places which are on the opposite side of the world.

appropriate, to take something for oneself as if it were one's own.

Ash Wednesday, the first day of Lent, the Christian fast.

aside, (spoken) so that the other actors on the stage are not supposed to hear.

ass, donkey.

attribute, a quality which naturally belongs to a person or a thing.

awe, respect mixed with some fear.

B

bait, (n.) the food put on a hook to catch fish with; (v.) to catch fish in this way.

bankrupt, one who cannot pay his debts.

bar, to exclude from consideration.

barbarous, cruel and uncivilized.

baron, a nobleman.

bastard, not genuine.

bated, held back (*with bated breath* – holding back one's breath through excitement).

beget, (past participle *begotten*) to become the father of.

behold, to look at.

bellow, to roar.

bereave (past participle *bereft*), to take away.

beseech, to ask earnestly.

bet, to promise money (or something else) to a person if he is right and you are wrong.

bid, to say something (as a greeting); to order.

bleat, to cry (of a sheep or goat).

blend, to mix.

blink, to open and shut one's eyes quickly.

bliss, great happiness.

blot, to dirty, stain.

bond, a written agreement about money.

bonnet, a hat.

bosom, the heart, the breast.

brag, to boast.

braggart, a boaster.

broth, water in which meat has been boiled.

burnished, polished, bright.

C

cackle, the cry of a hen or goose.

caper, to jump about in play

carcase, the dead body of an animal.

carrion, (dead) meat; of the flesh.

casement, a window opening from one side.

casket, a small box used for holding something precious.

casualty, accident.

chaff, the outer covering of grain, not used for food.

charter, an official paper giving certain rights, e.g. freedom and independence to a city.

chaste, pure.

cherub (plural, sometimes, *cherubin*), an imaginary child of great beauty, with wings on its shoulders.

cite, to mention as a proof.

clamber, to climb with difficulty, using the hands as well as the feet.

clown, a man who makes people laugh by telling jokes and behaving foolishly.

cobweb, the fine net made by a spider.

coffin, the box in which a dead person is buried.

colt, a young male horse.

competency, enough money to live on in comfort.

complexion, the natural appearance of the face.

compulsion, the state of being forced to do something.

concord, agreement, harmony.

confiscate, to take someone's property from him as a punishment.

congregate, to come together at the same time and place.

conjure, to compel, as if by magic.

constant, unchanging.

controversy, a difference of opinion.

cornet, a trumpet-like musical instrument.

corrupt, bad, in a bad state.

couch, a bed.

courteous, polite.

cozen, to deceive.

crave, to ask earnestly for.

cuckold, a man whose wife deceives him.

cudgel, (v.) to beat with a short, thick stick; (n.) such a stick used for beating.

cur, a worthless dog.

curb, to restrain.

currish, like a *cur.*

curtsey, to make a respectful greeting by bending the body and the knees.

D

dagger, a pointed knife used as a weapon.

decease, to die.

decree, an order given by a court.

demure, modest, quiet and serious.

destiny, fate.

detain, to keep back.

device, a plan.

devise, to think out.

dismay, fear of loss or disaster.

dispatch, to send off quickly.

divine, a priest.

242

dote on, to love deeply and un-questioningly.

dread, (v.) to fear; (n.) awe.

drone, a lazy person who lives on the earnings of others.

dross, anything which is generally considered to be worthless; non-precious metal, or the useless matter that rises to the surface when metal is melted.

E

ecstacy, very great pleasure.

edifice, a large building.

eloquence, fine, effective speaking.

enchant, to charm.

endeavour, effort.

engender, to produce.

enjoin, to command.

entreat, to beg earnestly.

ewe, a female sheep.

exact, to demand and get.

excrement, waste matter from the body, e.g. hair.

exhortation, an earnest request or warning.

exploit, a brave or adventurous act.

exposition, a detailed explanation.

F

famished, extremely hungry.

fang, a long, sharp, pointed tooth.

fawn, to try to win favour by acting towards others in a flattering way (as a dog might show pleasure by jumping up and licking the hands of its master).

fence, to fight with long, thin swords.

ferry, a place where a boat regularly carries people across a short stretch of water.

fleece, the woolly covering of a sheep.

flourish, a loud passage of music played to announce the arrival of an important person.

flint, a kind of very hard stone.

font, a stone basin in a church for holding the holy water used in baptism.

forfeit, (n.) something taken away as a punishment for an offence; (v.) to take, taken, in this way.

fray, a fight.

furnish, to provide (with something needed).

G

gallows, a wooden framework used for hanging criminals.

gambol, a jump or dance like a lamb's.

gaol, a public prison.

gape, to stare with the mouth wide open.

gaudy, showy, brilliant but without good taste.

gauge, to measure, judge.

gentile, a person who is not a Jew.

giddy, dizzy, feeling unable to stand firmly.

gild, to cover with gold.

ginger, the hot-tasting root of a certain plant, used as a flavouring or a sweetmeat.

glean, to gather the seeds left behind in the harvest field when the workers have finished.

gnat, a small flying insect.

godfather, a man who promises at the baptism of a child that he will help to teach the child about religion, morals, etc.

gondola, a light boat with high pointed ends, as used on the canals of Venice.

gormandize, to eat very greedily.

gratis, free, without charge.

graze, (of animals) to feed on growing grass.

Grecian, Greek.

gross, the whole amount.

grudge, a feeling of hatred.

guile, deceit.

gust, a sudden rush (of wind).

H

habitation, a place for people to live in.

halter, a rope used for hanging people.

hazard (n.), a game at dice with complicated chances; a choice which may get one a prize.

hazard (v.), to risk.

Hebrew, a Jew.

heinous, very wicked.

herb, a small plant of the kind used for making medicines and flavouring for food.

hermit, a person who leads a holy life by living alone and far away from other people.

hive, (n.) a place for bees to live in; (v.) to live in such a place.

ho!, a cry to call people's attention.

hollow, to shout.

hood, (to use) a cloth covering for the head and neck.

hoop, a circle of metal.

huddle, to press down in a mass.

hue, a colour, or shade of colour.

hug, to press tightly in the arms.

hymn, a religious song.

I

icicle, a piece of ice which hangs in a point.

idiot, a stupid person.

immure, to shut up within walls.

impart, to pass on to someone.

impediment, something that hinders.

impenetrable, what cannot be pierced.

importunity, earnest request, persuasion.

imposition, a troublesome command.

impugn, to attack by questioning.

inevitable, certain to happen.

inexorable, impossible to be turned aside.

infidel, a person who does not believe in Christianity.

infinite, endless.

infuse, to cause to pass into.

ingratitude, want of thankfulness.

injunction, a court order that something shall or shall not be done.

inscription, words stamped or cut on some hard material.

intercessor, one who intercedes, i.e. pleads or acts on behalf of someone else.

interior, the inside.

interpose, to put between, so as to hinder.

interpreter, one who explains.

issue, (1) a child, children; (2) the result of something.

ivory, the hard white substance which forms the tusks (long teeth which stick out when the mouth is closed) of animals, e.g. the elephant.

J

jaundice, a disease which causes the skin to turn yellow; it is accompanied by an unhappy state of mind.

jet, a hard, black mineral which polishes brightly.

jot, a very small amount.

K

kinsman, a male relative.

knave, a dishonest person.

L

leisure, free time in which one may rest, enjoy oneself, etc.

lewd, indecent.

limp, to walk lamely.

linger, to stay behind at a place or be slow in leaving it.

liver, the large, reddish-brown organ of the body which helps to digest food and purify the blood.

livery, a special dress worn by servants of a great house, usually with some mark to show who the servant belongs to.

locks, portions of hair which hang together.

lottery, a way of giving a prize by chance, e.g. by choosing one of many objects or numbers.

lyre, a kind of harp.

M

malice, the wish to do harm to others.

manifest, shown plainly.

mansion, a large, grand house.

mar, to spoil.

martlet, a bird like a swallow. Shakespeare seems to use *martlet* for *house-martin*, a bird of the swallow family which builds a nest of mud high up on the outside walls of houses.

masque, a kind of short play with music and dancing, for which the actors wore fine costumes.

mate, a partner.

meagre, thin, poor.

melancholy, sad; sadness.

mercenary, acting only for money or some other reward.

mesh, a net.

mincing, trying to be very delicate or refined in speech or movement (and therefore appearing foolish).

miscarry, to go wrong, meet with disaster.

monarch, a ruler, e.g. a king or emperor.

mortify, to overcome the desires and feelings of the body by discipline and self-denial.

mule, an animal half donkey and half horse.

N

neigh, to make the cry of a horse.

notary, a public official with some legal authority, e.g. the power to witness important papers.

notwithstanding, however; in spite of (what has just been said).

nourish, to feed.

nuptial, of weddings.

nymph, a lesser goddess; a beautiful girl.

O

oath, a sworn promise or statement.

obdurate, hard-hearted.

oracle, a person of great wisdom. In classical times an oracle was the answer given by a priest, who was believed to have been inspired by a god, to a question asked about the future.

oration, a formal speech.

orb, a ball-shaped object.

outrageous, shocking, bad beyond all reasonable limits.

P

pagan, one who worships false gods.

page, a boy who attends a person of high rank.

pageant, a grand public display which might take the form of a drama or a procession.

paltry, of no importance.

parrot, a tropical bird with a hooked beak and gaily coloured feathers. Parrots can often be taught to imitate human speech.

party, a person or group of people on one side in a legal action.

peal, a loud ringing, or sounding out.

peevish, frequently complaining.

penalty, a punishment for breaking the law.

penance, a punishment which is borne as a sign that one is sorry for some misdeed.

penthouse, a shed attached to a building.

peril, danger.

perjury, telling a lie when one has sworn to tell the truth.

pertain to, to belong to, be naturally concerned with.

pied, with various colours in patches.

pier, a breakwater; a structure built out into the sea or a river for use as a landing-stage.

pilgrimage, a journey made to a sacred place.

pine, an evergreen tree with leaves shaped like needles.

plea, an appeal.

pluck, to pull out, off, or from.

pork, the flesh of the pig used as food.

prate, to talk foolishly.

precedent, a previous case which is taken as justifying an action.

predicament, a difficult situation.

presage, to foretell.

principal, a sum of money on which interest is paid.

prodigal, a person who spends money wastefully.

prop, a support placed under or against something to hold it up.

pry, to look into something in an over-curious and unwelcome way.

puny, small and weak.

Q

quest, a search.

R

rack, an instrument of torture. (See *torture* below.)

rail, to complain angrily.

ram, a male sheep.

ratify, to confirm and approve.

ravenous, very hungry.

recant, to take back a statement which one has formerly made.

redeem, to save (a person) or get back (a thing) by payment.

relent, to begin to soften, show a little mercy.

render, to give.

rent, torn.

repent, to be full of regret for.

reproach, blame.

requite, to give in return, repay.

reverend, deserving respect.

rigorous, stern.

rite, a religious ceremony, or the form such a ceremony takes.

rivet, to fix together, as with a metal bolt.

rouse, to disturb (a person) into action.

S

sabbath, the holy day of the week.

scarf, a long piece of cloth worn round the neck.

sceptre, a staff carried by a ruler on great occasions as a sign of his power.

schedule, a written list.

scimitar, a short curved sword.

scripture, sacred writing.

scroll, a roll of paper with writing on it.

sepulchre, a place of burial.

serpent, a snake.

sever, to separate.

shed, to let fall (e.g. tears, blood).

shrew, a bad-tempered woman.

shrive, to hear someone's confession and, under certain conditions, pronounce God's forgiveness to him.

shrug, a slight lift of the shoulders.

shudder, to tremble (with fear or disgust).

shun, to keep away from.

singe, to burn slightly.

skull, the bone framework of the head.

slander, a false statement about a person which is made to do him harm.

slaughter, killing.

slay (past tense *slew*, past participle *slain*), to kill.

slink, to move in a guilty way, showing that one is ashamed.

smith, a man who works in iron, e.g. makes and fits horseshoes.

sole, the bottom of a shoe.

solely, only.

solemnize, to carry out (a ceremony) in the proper way.

specify, to state clearly and in detail.

sponge, an animal framework found in the sea which soaks up water.

spurn, to push away disgustedly with the foot.

squeal, to give a high, sharp cry.

stray, to wander.

streak, a stripe.

strumpet, a wicked woman.

stubborn, determined, refusing to change one's opinions.

substitute, a person or thing which takes the place of another person or thing.

suit, a claim taken to a law-court.

suitor, a man who is wooing a woman.

sunder, to separate.

superfluity, more than what is needed.

surety, one who promises to pay someone else's debts if this other person fails to pay.

surfeit, (to cause) to take too much of something.

surgeon, a doctor who does operations.

sway, rule.

synagogue, a building where Jews meet for worship.

T

tawny, brownish yellow.

tedious, long and dull.

temple, (1) the flat part on either side of the head between the forehead and the ear; (2) a building used for religious purposes.

temporal, worldly, not to do with the spirit or the life hereafter.

tender, to offer in payment.

thaw, to melt.

threshold, a doorstep.

thrice, three times.

thrift, care in spending money.

thrive, to prosper.

throstle, a thrush (a kind of bird with brown spots on its breast).

thwart, to oppose, bring to nothing.

tickle, to touch a person lightly, making him shiver or move sharply, and laugh.

torch, a flaming light on a stick.

torture, to cause a person great pain.

treason, the betrayal of a trust, e.g. siding with the enemy against one's own country.

treble, to make three times as large.

tribute, a forced payment.

trifle, (n.) something of little value or importance; (v.) to waste something as if it were of no importance.

turquoise, a blue precious stone.

twinkle (of the eye), to wink.

U

unbated, not held back or controlled.

unhallowed, cursed.

urine, the waste liquid discharged from the body.

usurer, a person who practises *usury*.

usury, the practice of lending money for interest (usually with the suggestion that the interest charged is unreasonably high).

utter, speak.

V

valiant, brave.

varnish, a hard, bright coating, sometimes covering up weaknesses within.

vehement, with strong feeling.

vein, one of the tubes along which the blood flows in the body.

vendible, suitable for selling.

vile, very bad.

villain, a bad man.

visage, the face (of a human being).

void, empty.

voluntary, (done) of one's own free will.

W

waft, to wave, carry lightly through the air.

wag, to move from side to side.

wager, a bet (see *bet*).

wand, a thin stick.

wanton, wild.

warranty, authority.

wedlock, the state of being married.

whet, to sharpen.

whirlpool, a place in the sea or a river where the water turns round in a circle with great force.

wilderness, a wild, deserted area of country.

wit, in *to wit,* namely.

woo, to make love to and ask for (a woman) in marriage.

woven, past participle and adjective of *weave.*

wren, a small bird.

wring (past tense *wrung*), to clasp warmly.

wrinkle, a line, e.g. in the face, made by a small fold or ridge.

wrought, another form of *worked.*